''This is a gentle and gallant narrative. These personal poignant memories paint universal pictures of growing up in rural America and struggling for economic security in the days of the Great Depression . . . joy in knowing people throughout the U.S., England, and Europe gives this journal its charm and unique quality.''

> Catherine Lauris
> University of Oregon Publications Editor
> Emeritus, Eugene, Oregon

''A remarkable woman tells her unusual life story in an honest, straight-forward way. A very reliable book. . . . Her recollections of the small town of Cooksville, Illinois in the early 1900s give life to history and are of signifi-cant historic value.''

> Jean McCrossin
> McLean County Historical Society,
> Bloomington, Illinois

The Hitchhiking Grandmother

''Grace Small's life is a unique recounting of the experiences of a woman who refused to conform . . . long before the women's movement. . . . Grace Small lived her own life in her own way . . . an entertaining . . . likeable personality.''

> Pepper Allen Berkeley
> Freelance writer, author, *Eugene Register-Guard*
> reporter 1959-1965, Portland *Oregonian* reporter
> and photographer 1966-1973, Vida, Oregon

''Ruth Davis has finally captured for us the twinkle in the eye of 'That' Grace who always challenged us to find some historical fact or something she had discovered on her latest trip. . . . It is selfish of us to think that with this memoir on our shelves 'Our Grace' is back in the Eugene Public Library forever . . . she belongs to the world . . . just as the world belonged to her.''

> Svea Gold
> Reference Librarian, Eugene Public Library
> Eugene, Oregon

''. . . an intriguing story of a most remarkable lady.''

> Ked Dejmal
> Science instructor, Spencer Butte Middle School,
> Eugene, Oregon

''Grace Small is an inspirational example of living life to the fullest. The lives she has touched in Jesus' name will never be the same.''

> Michael L. Rhoads
> Mathematics instructor, Willamette High School,
> Eugene, Oregon

Cabin Fever—1924

Would it be very wrong for a married woman who has a good husband and four nice children to leave the housework to her mother and work in an office?

Housework is not a success. The details are not important or else are neglected. Papering, painting, repairing, outside work, meeting people and seeing new things always seem of greater importance than whether there is dust under the piano or finger prints on the window pane.

All members of the family are sure that I cannot do anything well.

If I can learn to cook, to sew anything from fine embroidery to winter coats, to stay with a quilt until it is pieced, quilted, bound and folded away—if old white elephants ranging from broken beds to doll dressers can be repaired and used—all when every effort was a drive—surely it is possible for me to do the work I desire.

For nineteen years everything I wanted very badly came to me or I went to it. I was literally a boy—doing a man's work among men. In public work—meeting different people. Variety—always variety.

For thirteen years I have tried to be a faithful wife and conscientiously see after the children. I have never felt competent to do either. Surely there has been a fair trial.

Always there is the thought and desire to be among men—not as men but as fellow workers at things I understand.

Quite likely I couldn't get the work—there is a chance I wouldn't care for it again after all these years. But until I try and know there is a restlessness.

The work I want or think I want is nothing to be proud of or to want for a life work. It simply is to have charge of the repair parts for automobiles in connection with the garage work. It thrills me to hear a powerful motor running smoothly. To know every lock washer and cotter pin is right and all things adjusted correctly. While to be able to cook roast chicken, dressing, whipped potatoes, biscuits, gravy and apple pie is alright, only in fifteen minutes there is nothing but dirty dishes to show for all of it. Dishes to be washed, quarrels to be settled, chickens to be fed, floors swept, beds made—always over and over and over. Seeing no one day in and day out. Hearing nothing new. Same. Same. Same.

Would it be shirking a lifetime job I agreed on just to be away for the hours the family were away?

The Hitchhiking Grandmother

By
"That" Grace Small

As Told To
Ruth Barton Davis

With Best Wishes,
Ruth Barton Davis

THE PILGRIM WAY PRESS
1990

Available from:

The Pilgrim Way Press
Ruth Barton Davis
R.F.D. 1, Box 398 Thatcher Road
Forest Grove, Oregon 97116

—and—

The Pilgrim Way Press
Ruth Barton Davis
P.O. Box 584
Clinton, Maine 04927

International Standard Book Number: 0-9623785-0-X

Library of Congress Cataloging-in-Publication Data

Davis, Ruth Barton, 1920-
    The hitchhiking grandmother / by Ruth Barton
Davis.
        p.   cm.
    1. Davis, Ruth Barton, 1920- —Journeys.
2. United States—Description and travel.   3. Europe—
Description and travel.   4. Hitchhiking—United States.
5. Hitchhiking—Europe.   6. Grandmothers—United
States—Biography.   I. Title.

CT275.D2842A3   198989-16289
917.304'92—dc20   CIP

Cover Photo Credit:
Lompoc Record, Lompoc, California, January 18, 1966

Cover and Book Design: Mary Wilson

Printed by:

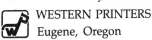 WESTERN PRINTERS
Eugene, Oregon

Dedication

This book is dedicated to my
relatives, friends and strangers in this country and abroad
in whose homes I received much gracious hospitality.
And it is especially dedicated to the
hundreds of men and women drivers who stopped
to give a ride to a "hitchhiking grandmother."
To all of them—
one last hearty "Thank you, kindly."

—"That" Grace Small

Acknowledgments

My thanks to all who labored with me and who provided encouragement and information toward the completion of this book. This includes family, friends, editors, and those who simply took the time to listen.

There are some who contributed in very special ways:

- —Linda Hacheney, who introduced me to Grace Small.
- —Margaret Minor, Adrith Wirkus, Edna Glines and Mary Acamo, my peers from the Eugene Public Library's Writers Support Group.
- —Penny Allmett, a typist with constant effervescence.
- —Marjorie Helfrich, Dick Helfrich and Dr. and Mrs. Allen Boyden, who provided information about camping on the Rogue River.
- —Judi and Karl Wyssen, who supplied pertinent information about a locale in Switzerland.
- —Eugene Public Library Reference Department.
- —University of Oregon Library Reference and Map Departments.
- —James and Susan Davis, who edited and greatly encouraged me.
- —Mary Ann Wilson, my printer, who not only took on this project professionally, but also put her talents, imagination and heart into it and pleased the writer with whom she worked.

And, most of all, Grace Small, who spent so much time over the years meticulously preparing her albums and manuscripts for the eventual publication of her story.

Ruth Barton Davis

Contents

Preface

I was born in McLean County, Illinois and spent more than a third of my life in that area.

I think of my life as three lives. Each was distinctively different from the other. For that reason I have written my autobiography in three parts.

The first was in Illinois: Cooksville where I grew up and Bloomington where I reared my four children. The second was when I went to live in the West. The third was hitchhiking. I possessed an insatiable appetite to travel. I liked geography and history, and I knew I would never have enough money to travel conventional ways. When I retired, hitchhiking was a way to get where I wanted to go. I hitchhiked for 27 years, at least 19 times across the United States and 10 trips through the West coast states alone.

In my eighties, I had a fall and two small strokes. After the age of 86, I faced the fact that hitchhiking was over. Besides, the changes in our times dictated there was nothing safe about it. (No one should think that because I was unscathed, they would be preserved from harm.)

I have had over 90 years of living, and I have lived every day to the fullest. I sometimes acted foolheartedly, but I like to believe that mostly I acted wisely. I profited by my experiences, and I hope you will, in some way, profit by them, too.

"That" Grace

Footloose—May 31, 1947

Home in Bloomington, Illinois, was not home anymore. My aged mother had recently died, my father years before. Children and grandchildren were scattered; life was empty. I was 51 years old.

Encouraged by friends on the West Coast, I decided to go to California and start life over again. By hitchhiking, I figured my life savings of $64 would get me there.

Hitchhiking was illegal in Illinois so I took a bus to St. Louis, Missouri, where friends, Mr. and Mrs. D. E. Pings, took me in for a few days. Because I yearned to take a riverboat ride down the Mississippi, we visited several riverboat line companies, but their sternwheelers had already gone. The price was also beyond my means.

Cold facts brought me to my senses. Leaving my friends, I set out hitchhiking.

Except for my little black suitcase, I didn't look like a hitchhiker. I was dressed in a light blue suit and wore a matching hat. Three rides took me as far as Cuba, Missouri, which was out of my way. I got a hotel room for the night and planned how to get back on my route.

The following night I was in Tulsa, Oklahoma. The next morning my ride was in a lovely new Buick with a New Mexico license. It couldn't have been better because the driver was going to Roswell where I planned to see one of my daughters.

Near midnight, he set my suitcase on her porch. Eileen and my grandson Jimmy were taken by surprise. I stayed a week to visit and to orient. One pleasure trip with Jimmy and his friend, Bobby Richardson, to Carlsbad Caverns filled, for a while, the void within me.

But I left Roswell to go to visit another daughter stationed with her husband in Albuquerque. It was very hot when I took the city bus to the edge of town and put up my thumb. After waiting an hour, I was tempted to turn back and ask Eileen for bus fare. She had wanted me to let her give it rather than see me hike.

Exhausted from the heat, I took the first ride offered. The car was a dark color and dusty. There were three in the front seat, an older man, his son and his grandson. They were casually dressed, and the younger man opened the back door for me. They were on their way to Albuquerque.

At first, there was the usual conversation, but when they began to speak in a language I didn't understand, I became apprehensive. When they became argumentative and angry with each other, I was frightened. However, I passed it off as a family matter and hoped it would end.

We stopped for gas at Ramon, New Mexico, which was the only station along a 60-mile stretch of desert. The older man took his grandson with him and headed for the tavern to get a beer. The younger man stayed to tend the car. He walked over to my window and I rolled it down.

In a constrained tone, he politely begged my pardon. "I don't like what my father is planning," he said. Then he insisted that I should, "Make a real effort to get another ride. When we get back, you be gone."

I didn't have to ask questions. The urgency of his speech caused me to grab my suitcase and swish away to the highway as fast as I could.

It made no difference to me which way the next car was going. I would take a ride in any direction to escape whatever awaited me.

As I stood, I tried to surmise what my danger was. Robbery? I wore a nice watch, earrings, and a ring. It might have been my suitcase or my purse, though I had little money. Perhaps a beer mixed with bad driving would have endangered all our lives. There was also the possibility of harm to my person.

It had only been five minutes, but I felt like I had waited hours when a truck stopped. I climbed in, weak and trembling. This was a good ride. The driver took me all of the way to the Air Force base in Albuquerque. My safe arrival made me most grateful. But, beyond that, I knew this was only half of the way I had to go. The West Coast was still a long way off.

PART I

The Horse Knows the Way

Looking down from imaginary heights (for there are no real heights to look from) onto the crossroads that part the spreading fields of grain in McLean County, Illinois, one can visualize horses pulling a wagon or a horse bearing the weight of its rider. Reins in hand, the drivers direct the horses. But, even if the drivers did not use the reins, the horses would know the way to go. All is quiet.

The scene changes. Through one of the roadways, a cloud of dust makes its way; destined, the sound of a gasoline powered motorcar breaks the calm.

CHAPTER ONE

The Beginning of the Williamses

". . . a time to be born . . ."
—Ecclesiastes 3:2 (KJV)

I was born a Williams in the year 1895. There were three of us: Mother, Dad, and I. Our lives entwined until my parents died. It is important to tell about them.

Mother was a favored child. Her father, Richmond Curl Mills, owned a flourishing grist and sawmill at the bend of Pittman's Creek in Somerset, Kentucky. Shortly before her birth, her father was killed in an accident at the mill. Her widowed mother found alleviation from grief in her newly born daughter; she gave her her own first name, Sarah, and her father's name, Richmond. She was called Richa.

My mother was spoiled and allowed to play while others did the housework and chores. She grew to be an attractive woman and wore expensive clothes. She wrote her long red hair piled on top of her head.

She had many suitors as a young woman and broke a few hearts before she married. She told me when I was older that the Devil owed her a debt and paid it with the Williams family.

My dad, Richard L. Williams, was one of ten children. His family were hunters and lived from hand to mouth. Their home was a log cabin on Sugar Hill near Somerset. No one was a stranger to them.

With a dimple in his chin and mischief in his eyes, my dark haired,

3

The Mills family at the old Kentucky home on Pitman Creek, built about 1846. My mother is on the left and Grandma Mills in the center. (1894)

mustached dad was a fine looking man. At 24, he loved a challenge and when he met Mother, he found one.

Brokenhearted over the death of a brother in Illinois where they were working, Dad came back to Somerset. Mother had recently quarreled with a boyfriend and saw an opportunity to make him jealous by playing up to Dad. Glad to have her sympathy, Richard became Richa's friend.

Friendship grew to romance. Though Mother was 12 years older, Dad asked her to marry him. He told her glowing stories of the rich farm land in Illinois, and said that people were making a very good living there. He was persuasive and they were married December 23, 1894. There was a ten-day infare celebration that combined Christmas and New Years. Peculiar to that region of the United States, family and friends packed up and came long distances to have a part of the festivities.

The Mills home was built in the early 1800s. Through the years, it had become a triplex, having been added onto to accommodate the new young couples in the family. It housed many of the wedding guests.

The celebration ended, and my parents were taken with their trunks to the depot where they boarded a train for Merna, Illinois, a small district in McLean County, 500 miles away.

Mother left a warm loving family behind. For three days and three nights they listened to the clacking of the wheels on the steel rails. Mother's heart was mingled with joy and sadness.

When they arrived, Dad learned there was no work until spring, but they were given shelter and provisions on the Elvin farm where he was scheduled to work.

Mother wanted to make friends, but the people there were clannish, not like Kentuckians. Also, she wore silk and satin dresses, while the other women wore cottons and calicos. They thought she considered herself to be better than they were.

When Mother learned she was pregnant, matters complicated. At 36, she was old to be having her first child. Morning sickness, along with the changes that came over her once slim and beautiful figure, were hard to accept.

Depressed, she sat looking out across the snow-covered fields. It was the most flat, monotonous land she had ever seen. Once she crawled under the table and covered her head to shut away reality. She did not anticipate the future.

My birth was a painful struggle for her. I appeared red, scrawny and ugly. Wrapped, I weighed five pounds.

Because Mother could not nurse, and cows milk did not agree with me, Dad sent out for someone to bring mare's milk. When it arrived, Dad added a "drap," as he would say it, of whiskey to give it more substance. So it was that I became my dad's "boy," September 21, 1895. He called me "Gracie."

When I got too big to be wrapped in blankets, Mother wanted to make a dress for me. Yardage was not available in McLean County and, anyway, she had no money. She rummaged through her silk and satins, but the only garment suitable for a baby dress was a lovely white, patented cotton apron. She cut and stitched a beautiful ruffled dress for me. I treasured the dress for more than 80 years because, in spite of how my birth seemed to have affected my mother, it convinced me that she loved me.

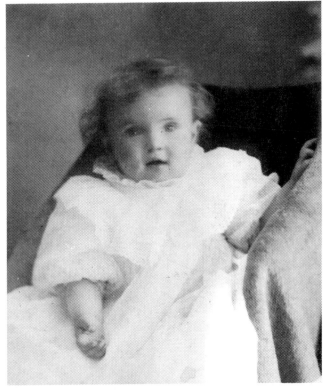

This is my dress and this is my right thumb.

CHAPTER TWO

A Little Bit of Farming

". . . A well of water springing up. . . ."
—John 4:14 (KJV)

By the time I was five I had moved five times within Blue Mound Township. Three of the moves were to farms.

The first was onto the White's place where we lived in a beautiful, grand, two-story house. The outstanding feature of the place was an artesian well on the lawn near the road. The road had once been an Indian trail, and scouts led wagon trains to the watering hole. The water was so deep that barrels could be lowered and filled to the brim.

When we lived there, people still stopped for water. I made a point to see who came. People and animals were always thirsty when they got that far. When a highway was built to replace the road in 1930, it saddened me that the well was covered and the stream diverted. However, for an historical marker a huge white rock was placed where the water once surfaced.

The White farm was also in a waterfowl migration route and was popular with hunters. Each time, when the hunters left, there were empty shotgun shells lying around. The owner's little grandson and I picked them up to play with on the lawn. We built houses, villages, and forts. He was my first playmate.

During the daytime, Dad kept an eye on me from across the field while Mother was doing housework. It was drudgery to her to prepare meals, clean house and do laundry. Dad's clothes smelled like cows, hogs, and horses. Life had come down hard on her. She never expected married life would be like it was. Her gorgeous silks and satins became housedresses, and her former vivacious self crawled into a shell to emerge only in the presence of a few chosen friends. In spite of it all, there was a certain strength that kept her going.

Dad was such a hard worker that farmers were anxious to hire him, so we never knew where we would be. For myself, I was glad that, when we moved from the Whites, the next farm had chickens. Chickens were my favorite animal, and I made a pet out of one of their hens. She had a personality that stood out from all of the others.

We were on the Burbanks' farm. One day during corn harvest Mother and Dad were in the field picking and throwing ears into a wagon pulled by a team of horses. My hen and I followed along behind. Turning one way and then another she scratched and pecked out food to her heart's content. I took pleasure in watching her as she went between the stocks.

Finally, I decided to get into the wagon and watch from there. I was settling myself on the back of the wagon when the horses spooked and started to run away. Though I was not frightened, my father was. He took off running after the team and didn't see my pet chicken. With all his weight his foot came down on her and crushed her. I do not remember how he stopped the horses, but I cried for a long time because he had killed my chicken.

On Sunday afternoons farmers came to have Dad cut their hair. These men, I noticed, had interesting things to talk about. Sometimes it was gossip and sometimes news. One week the talk was about some farmland at the Rosebud Indian Reservation in South Dakota. According to Ed Sutor, a landowner in McLean County, some of the land had been opened for sale. Ed wanted to see it and wanted Dad to go with him. Dad agreed.

When Mother heard about it, she wanted to go along. If there was going to be a change in her life, she wanted to know what it entailed. She had come to Illinois trusting Dad to provide for her in the manner to which she was accustomed, but found herself working the same as any hired man's wife. This time she wanted to know in advance what she would be getting into. But, Dad didn't include her, and I never knew why.

When Dad got back, he had taken land. Because Mother refused

Dad promised to bring me a present.

to go to a place she hadn't seen, he had to forfeit it. Like Mother, I was disappointed that Dad didn't take me to South Dakota, too. I wanted to ride the train.

"I'll bring you a present, Gracie," he said. Dad brought me a piece of an Indian headdress. It was a strip of leather covered with beads of many colors and in the center it had a beaded star. It also had a fringe on the ends made of porcupine quills. Each quill was intricately set into the next and strung on fine sinew. It made a clacking sound when the quills struck together. This pleased me, but it was the beads that Dad thought that I would enjoy. I took some off and tried to string them, but I couldn't find a needle small enough to go through the beads.

There was also a mystery about the piece of leather. It was scorched and slightly curled on one side. The Rosebud Indians had a custom of burning the belongings of their deceased, so I have wondered if the piece of headdress was snatched from the fire, or was it found near the place of burning? I learned about the custom too late to ask my father how he acquired my gift.

Though the Sunday barber shop was a brief period in my life, through it I acquired an insatiable appetite for gossip and the artful method of eavesdropping.

When Dad's work on the Burbank place ended, we moved to the Barkers' farm, and new experiences began.

Jesse Barker came from England when the flat, vacant land of Illinois was opened to homesteaders. He brought his family, and not only did he get land for himself, he got adjoining land for each of his children. However, they were unable to have fences and their cattle got into the grain. Fence posts and barbed wire were too costly because they had to be shipped by rail. Jesse remembered the beautiful hedges that graced the borders of the farms in England and decided to grow some hedges to serve as fences. He hunted for a proper plant and thought that bodark (Osage Orange) would serve the purpose. He stuck cuttings into the ground all around his property and did the same for his sons' land.

In no time, the cuttings grew into gangling bushes full of sharp thorns. Barker was disappointed. The hedges did not, in any way, resemble the ones he knew in his homeland.

Determined to win out, he had special knives made like machetes and hired men trimmed the plants into hedges. Because the prunings were full of thorns, they had to be hauled away and burned.

Before long the bushes sprouted shoots and were out of control again. Barker conceded that the whole effort was unprofitable and had the hedges removed. He left a few plants equal distances apart to trim and use as fence posts. When he could afford it, he purchased barbed wire and made a proper fence.

My favorite way of passing time on the Barker place was watching the trains. A spur of the Illinois Central Railroad ran along one border of the land near our house. When I heard a train, I ran out to wave to the trainmen. In time, they took me on the train with them the five miles to Fletcher to switch cars.

When I lived at the Burbank farm, I acquired two chicks. I carried them around in a strawberry basket. One was a white hen and the other a black Plymouth Rock rooster. I took them on the train with me because I thought, since I enjoyed it, they probably would, too. I am sure the trainmen were amused.

Our next move was to the little town of Cooksville.

CHAPTER THREE

The Hotel

"In my prosperity I said I shall never be moved."
—*Proverbs 30:6 (KJV)*

Though Dad spent much of his time working on farms, his heart was not in farming. If any other job was available, he took it. Opportunity came for him when he was asked by a landowner, Wes Woodard, to manage a hotel for him in Cooksville. It was near the depot and was built to accommodate tourists, salesmen, and trainmen. Former managers were not business oriented nor willing to work, so the hotel was idle. Wes was sure Dad could make a go of it.

Dad's only experience in a hotel was when he went to South Dakota and was a guest; but I heard Wes make the offer and Dad accept. When Mother was informed we were moving into a hotel in Cooksville, it was news to her.

Dad was ideal for the job. He liked people and was handsome. Wearing a tie was his trademark, and he always wore a tie.

Mother's work was hardest. She made beds, cleaned, washed, did dishes, cooked and baked. Inexperienced, she had yet to learn to let the dough rise on the wood stove's hot water reservoir.

I was not old enough to help and was suppose to stay out of the way. Dad bought a square piano for me. It sat in the guest parlor and I took lessons for a while. But, since I didn't want to sit still, he let me quit.

There was a little girl named Verna Means who lived in a house down by one of the grain elevators. It was so noisy there that she liked to come to the hotel and play. We were allowed to do whatever

Hotel management suited Dad.

we wanted to as long as we did not disturb the guests, so we decided to act like mice.

We went into the dining room to the tables where there were cookies and crackers under cloth covers. We giggled as we put our heads under the corner of a cloth and ate cookies and crackers to our hearts' content. Afterward, the table was covered with crumbs for Mother to clean up.

Dad was proud of his hotel and wrote about it to his family in Kentucky. They thought it was so wonderful that in a short time all of them migrated to Cooksville. They moved into the hotel without paying for their rooms or their board. This was not what Dad had had in mind, but he was glad to see them and let them take what he thought was temporary residence. This upset Mother to say the least.

She kept the rooms for Dad's parents, his four brothers and their wives, and three unmarried sisters. She cooked and served their meals. She tried to be civil, but not one offered a hand to lightened her load.

Finally, she asked Dad to get some of them to help her. He passed the message on but none were inclined. Mother got agitated. Everyone was frightened the day she exploded. Dad's youngest sister,

Maggie, was in the guest parlor playing the piano for the Williams family. They were singing merrily in old Kentucky style. Maggie sang a lively folk song, "The Cat Came Back." The words flowed fast:

> Dar was ole Mister Johnson,
>   He had trouble of his own,
> He had an ole ya-ler cat
>   That wouldn't leave its home.
> He tried everything he knew
>   To keep the cat away . . .
> Eb-en sent it to the preacher
>   And told it for to stay.

Everyone was laughing at Maggie because she carried on so. Mother could hear it as she slaved in the kitchen. It was as if she were being mocked.

Maggie continued with gusto on the chorus. I watched her rolling her head around as she bellowed:

> But the cat came back
>   Couldn't stay no longer.
> Yes, the cat came back
>   The very next day.
> The cat came back,
>   Thought he was a gonner,
> But the cat came back,
>   It wouldn't stay away.

At Maggie's last word, my pretty red-haired mother, face burning with anger, stormed into the parlor. She held a large stove poker with both hands above her head. She swung it first toward one and then another as she screeched, "Get out of this hotel! Every one of you!"

Frightened, some of the Williamses froze where they stood; some backed toward the walls, not knowing what would happen next. Dad came to see what was going on. What he saw was Mother holding the poker as if to strike. Composed, he ushered his kin toward the doorway. That day the extra Williamses moved out.

They dispersed in several directions. Livery horses and buggies were brought to move my grandparents and my three single aunts to Wes Woodard's farm. My four uncles got wagons and buggies to move themselves and their wives to some of Wes's other farms.

As time passed my aunts married McLean County men. Aunt Maggie married a man named Felkamp in the town of Fletcher. He died and she later married a man named Harness. Aunt Mattie married the hotel keeper at the Green Hotel next to the train depot in Cooksville, and Aunt Molly married Charles Barker, one of Jesse Barker's sons.

After the great exodus, Dad went into the kitchen to help Mother. I once heard it said that when a man born and raised in Kentucky helps in the kitchen, he has been licked. At any rate, dinner was served to the hotel patrons on time that day, and in the usual formal manner. Mother didn't like housecleaning, but she did a pretty good job of it that day.

Change came for us again, and not by choice. One morning while everyone was asleep, Mother smelled smoke. The hotel was on fire. Dad roused the guests. In a two-story hotel, it didn't take long to alert them.

There was no fire department, and the loss was great. Beautiful china pitcher and washbowl sets were thrown out second-story windows in the panic, only to smash in pieces on the ground. Some immigrants from Switzerland and Germany had left valuable possessions locked in their rooms while they worked elsewhere, and no one could get to them to save them. Dad had received a large shipment of cigars a few days earlier, and they went up in smoke in their own boxes. The next day he got the bill for them.

We could not save the hotel furniture, but we got a little of our own. My beautiful piano burned, and I didn't realize at the time what I had lost.

The Crumbaker Hardware stood next to the hotel and its brick wall, smudged with smoke, stared back at us. Opposite was a heap of iron bedsteads and smoldering ashes. What we viewed conveyed a somber message. We had no place to live, and Dad needed a job. He had thought we were settled permanently, but we were forced to move again.

CHAPTER FOUR

Life with the Telephone Company

"Make me to know my end . . . that I may know how frail I am."
—Proverbs 39:4 (KJV)

Dad began to look for work. A manager's position was open at the Horton Hotel in Astoria across the Illinois River south and west of Bloomington. We went to see what it was like. I was filled with excitement when we boarded the train.

Dad and Mother both had jobs. Mother's was cooking and maid work again, but Dad was not a manager. The most important of his duties was to catch fish for the hotel.

He took me with him. We rode in a buggy to the river, and I was put in a boat that was moored there. Dad waded into the water. With a long, pronged fish spear called a gig, he captured the fish and tossed them into the boat. When the cold water splashed on me I flinched. I hated sitting in the boat with wet, flopping fish.

I had a playmate in Astoria. The hotel owner had a son about my age who was glad when he learned that I didn't play with dolls. At his suggestion, we rode make-believe horses using the head- and foot-board of a huge, ornately carved bed in one of the guest rooms. It struck me that it would be even better if we had guns to wave as we rode.

We climbed down and, feeling very smart, I led the way to Dad's dresser. I pulled open a drawer and took out Dad's two six shooters.

I carefully emptied the .45 caliber bullets from the guns the same way I had seen my father do it. Then I handed a gun to my friend, and we went back to ride our "horses." We whooped and hollered, urging our steeds onward.

Dad came to investigate. Terrified by what he saw as he entered the room, he spoke my name in a strained voice: "Gracie!"

We stopped and looked at him. He calmly asked for the guns which we obediently held out to him. When he learned they were not loaded, he was greatly relieved.

Our rides were over, and we shinnied down the bedposts. Dad gently pulled me close enough so he could look me in the eye, and the scolding he gave brought tears. He never had spanked me. This time I would have felt better if he had.

Three months in Astoria was long enough for Dad, and we returned to Cooksville.

When we got off the train, we were met by friends who were glad to have us home. We moved into the Green Hotel near the depot which was the hub of activity. It was a place to go to get news and, for Dad, a place to learn about work.

One day Dad and I were there, and we overheard two men from the telephone company talking about bringing lines to Cooksville so that the farmers could get grain prices earlier and know when to sell.

One of the men asked Dad if he would like a job with the company. Though Dad didn't know a transmitter from a receiver, he took the offer because it would mean long-term employment.

The equipment needed to hang the phone lines was not available so Dad made the climbing irons and spurs. He also made the safety harnesses.

Dad drove a team of horses that pulled a wagon loaded with poles and reels of wire. He, with his helpers, often worked in the extreme heat while heavy prairie winds blew dust in the air around them. Sometimes they worked in the rain and waded in mud. It was either dust or mud in McLean County.

It was the year 1901. I was six years old. Dad made sure I had some jobs along with him to keep me busy. He added more responsibility as I got older. One duty made me feel important. I was to help keep the telephones functioning. During electrical storms, carbon often collected inside a metal box on top of the telephone. I rode a bicycle to the homes to scrape off the carbon. Sometimes I had

Cooksville Telephone Company line men in the mud. My dad is on the left. (1909)

to ride quite a distance. I liked jobs that took me into homes.

Outside the telephone office and on top of a pole was a fuse box. When a line went out of order, it was my job to climb the pole and check the fuses. The operator cranked the voltage up, and I wet my finger and put it on a fuse. If my finger didn't get a tingling feeling, I knew which fuse to change. This chore was sometimes embarrassing because women didn't wear slacks then. Though my skirt was long, when I climbed, I showed my legs.

The telephone company had a new two-story building on Garfield Street. It was a 24-by-24-foot frame structure, and we lived on the second floor. It was divided into quarters. We had three rooms and the company had the fourth.

The first floor of the building served as the city hall. Fire equipment, voting booths and the jail each had their own compartment.

The jail was an iron, cagelike structure that sat on the floor. The top didn't reach the ceiling, and the very first prisoner escaped. As soon as he was left alone, he lifted the cage, supported it with the chamber pot, and crawled out. There were improvements made soon afterwards.

Once there was a fire in the livery stable next to the blacksmith shop. Fire equipment was brought, but I was one of the first to get there. Had I not been a tomboy, I would have been of no use. I helped blindfold the horses to lead them out. Unfortunately, there were not enough men and five or six animals were lost. The equipment from the fire station helped put out the fire, but it took people to save the horses.

The telephone office was cramped; the equipment filled every space leaving little room for the operator.

There was a switchboard and a swivel chair. Also, a soundproof cubical where people could make calls without disturbing the operator and, on a shelf close to the booth, were four gallons of hazardous blue vitrol (sulfuric acid) for use in the batteries.

The aisle was very narrow. Even so, at night a cot was placed there for the use of a crippled, high-school boy, Cleon Hayes, who took the late calls.

The telephone business did not grow locally as anticipated. Many of the immigrant farmers were not interested in owning one, or else they were afraid of them. During storms, lightning sometimes followed a phone line and caused a house fire; but grounding took care of that. Still, the telephone company needed some positive promotion to gain customers. One of the company men, Tom Powers, who was also the telegraph operator at the train depot, came up with an idea.

It was election year, 1904. Teddy Roosevelt was running for president. Tom knew the farmers were eager for the election results. He could get the returns by telegraph, so he arranged a gathering in the Odd Fellows Hall over Clatfelter's Store. The hall filled with men enthusiastic about the election, and Tom had a captive audience in regard to his soliciting business for the telephone company.

I got to see the whole show. Dad had me tally the votes, but I had to have help because they came in so fast. The cheering was loud when Roosevelt won. Smoking, chewing and spitting tobacco, the men were telling jokes and laughing loudly. Tom figured that if he was going to get in a word for the telephone company, he had better get their attention fast. He called out above the noise and asked them all to please sit down because he had something to say.

When they were seated, he proceeded to tell them about the telephone company, the need to learn about the grain markets early, and the safety and reliability of the telephone. When he got through, almost everyone signed up for an installation. Tom's plan had worked.

That night was an historic event for the nation and a great promotional for the Cooksville Telephone Company. There were miles and miles of phone lines hung after that eventful night.

It was not a comfortable place to live at the phone office. We had three rooms, but we used only two. I did not have a room of my own; I slept on a cot in the kitchen. It was also the dining room, washroom, and the room where we took our baths in a galvanized tub. There was not room for a stove larger than a two-burner kerosene model. Mother cooked our simple meals on it and the room always smelled of kerosene.

We ate in relays on a wooden wash stand. The "Hello Girl," as the operator was called, ate first. Then Dad and I ate. Mother waited on us. We were out and gone when she ate. We had no family life.

Mother and Dad's bedroom had the usual furnishings and some storage. But, there were also burglar alarms installed in their room. They were connected to the bank, a hardware store, and another business. My parents were to ring the owner and the police if one of the alarms sounded.

Our third room was to be kept pretty, but it was too close to the switchboard operator and any amount of noise was distracting. So we never used it.

There was much activity outside the building. The town pump was at the back and everyone came there to get water. Also, the town hitching posts were at the front. Horses were left there whenever anyone came to town.

There was about an acre of land at the rear that was used for a city park and recreation area. Every Saturday night there was entertainment there for the farmers. Occasionally, it was provided by the townspeople who arranged picnics, community sings, and ice cream socials. However, most of the entertainment was professional. The most popular events were the traveling medicine shows, carnivals that came in on the train, and dog-and-pony shows. Once, evangelist

Three telephone operators or "hello girls." The center one is my Aunt Maggie.

Billie Sunday came and held a tent meeting.

Living on the plains, we longed for variety. We didn't have radios nor did we have a movie theatre. My young cousin, Clifford Harness, brought a slide show for entertainment once. He had gotten the equipment through one of the hardware stores. Makeshift benches were placed in rows on the lot where our hotel had burned, and the pictures were projected onto the side of the Crumbaker building.

Clifford used a magic lantern powered by carbide. We all fancied that we had experienced our first picture show. My Aunt Maggie, Clifford's mother, came along to sing. Though the entertainment was not a Hollywood production, the evening was one of Cooksville's best events.

For all-around entertainment, the Cooksville crowds enjoyed the carnivals most. However, parents cautioned their children about associating with show people, and warned them not to speak to the carnival workers. That is, all did except mine. Either my parents never thought of it , or they knew it was unavoidable because the carnival was in our backyard.

I took advantage of the opportunity. Carnival folk let me ride the trained ponies, pet the show dogs, and hold puppies on my lap. I took racoons on leashes for a stroll. I saw the wardrobes in the carnival wagons, and I even ate strange food cooked on a wee little stove in one of the wagons.

Sometimes I was around the roustabouts who set up the tents. Some told jokes that I should not have heard, but that didn't faze me; I had always been around men and heard talk like that. These men had been "around" though . . . all around.

One night, I went on a date with a carnival laborer who was a real gentleman. It was the day I turned 16. Dad thought I was out with a young man who worked for us. When I came home, he learned the truth. After the young man left, he gave me my first and last spanking. He turned me over his lap and used a small horse whip on me. To me, it was more fun than punishment, because Dad was completely out of character. All the time he whipped me, I was laughing inside. I knew the young man I went out with was a "swell kid." We corresponded for a year after that.

When I was old enough, I filled in at the telephone switchboard, but I disliked the job. When things got boring, I listened in on the party lines. All operators did it, and we were probably the best-informed people around.

I got myself in trouble once because I thought I knew everything there was to know about a prize racehorse named Tanglefoot. His owner was a young man named Bill Lake who was an underdog sort of fellow and lived five miles from Cooksville on the Mackinaw River. Bill bought the horse from Dr. Nogle and often raced him illegally on the back roads.

One day Bill came to town with his friend, James Fossett, in a buggy pulled by Tanglefoot. He pulled in between two other buggies, fastened the reins to the rail, and hooked the checkrein. Then the two men crossed Garfield to John Shattler's restaurant to eat dinner.

I was watching from the telephone office. The day was hot, and the flies were thick. They lit on the horses, and the horses jerked their heads, shook their manes, and swished their tails—all but Tanglefoot. His tail was docked for racing and did him no good; neither could he toss his head because Bill had fastened the checkrein.

I pitied him as I watched the annoying flies. I thought, since he had no tail to switch, he should at least be able to toss his head to get some relief.

I went out to the hitching rail. As I approached Tanglefoot, he eyed me wildly and took a few short steps away. I reached up and unhooked the checkrein from the surcingle. Satisfied, I went back to the switchboard.

I didn't wait to see what happened after that, but I learned later that the horse could perform a trick which a tight checkrein prevented. Tanglefoot got his head down against the hitching rail and rubbed his bridle until it slipped off over his ears. Adroitly he backed keeping the buggy clear of those on either side. He took off racing for home with the buggy bouncing behind him.

Bill and James returned. The spot where they had parked the buggy was empty. The bridle dangled from the hitching post. Bill looked around, but didn't see his horse. He knew he had fastened the checkrein and was going to have some answers.

It didn't take him long to find me because of my reputation for always being in the middle of things and my proximity to the scene of the crime.

He stomped up the wooden stairs and thrust himself through the doorway. He fired his questions fast. I was so frightened I couldn't give answers.

My face grew hot with fear. The tongue-lashing he gave me left me helpless to speak for myself or his horse.

When he was through, he went out and stomped down the stairs. He and James had to walk in the hot sun five miles home. I was sorry for what I had done; I didn't know all I thought I knew.

I conclude that working for the telephone company could, on the whole, not be called dull.

CHAPTER FIVE

"That Williams Girl"

"Thou knowest my downsitting and my uprising . . ."
—Psalm 139:2 (KJV)

My reputation as a child could be summed up in a few words: "What will she think of next?"

For instance, I had a cat I loved. I named him Ted after President Roosevelt, and I expected a lot of him. Once I made a tiny harness with reins and hitched him to a little red wagon. I taught him to pull it down the street while I drove. On the Fourth of July I decorated the wagon and cat with red, white, and blue bunting, and joined the parade. But, Ted was independent, and when I wanted to harness him later, he ran away.

I tried a similar act with my pet chickens from the Burbanks' farm. I tied strings on their wings and drove them down the street. My hen soon wised up and became very hard to catch. Her favorite place to run was under the back porch out of my reach. Being outwitted by a hen was hard to take.

The rooster was different. He was a huge, beautiful Plymouth Rock. He loved to parade when I harnessed him. As I drove, he gloriously strutted up the boardwalk to crow in front of a chicken pen. Every house on the walk had a pen, so he always had an audience. The rooster inside the fence would crow to him, and mine would answer more robustly. The uproar made such a disturbance I had to pick up my rooster and move on to keep the owners from getting after me. At the next pen the scene was repeated. Some people pulled back their curtains to watch as if they enjoyed it. I got the rooster to pull the wagon several times, and we made a lasting impression on the residents of Cooksville.

The bank building was the scene of my wildest antics. There, I shocked the most proper people in town. Sometimes I walked my bicycle up the steps and rode with no hands onto the boardwalk below. When that goings-on was no longer daring enough, I rode the bicycle down backwards. Once I roller-skated down the bank steps. Other times I walked up and down on stilts. I purposed to have fun and get attention at the same time; I found I could do that best at the bank.

People didn't dare to cross me because I was always ready and able to fight. I often did. It didn't occur to me that as a girl, I shouldn't act that way. At least three boys, two girls and a woman received black eyes from me. Some folks got a mouthful of mud or a general "going over." They learned not to interfere with "that Williams girl."

In grade school I was a problem for the teacher. Once she caught me with my feet pulled up and crossed behind my head. She punished me by making me stay after school and memorize lines from James Russell Lowell's *The Vision of Sir Launful*. I have never forgotten it: "And what is so rare as a day in June? Then, if ever, come perfect days. . . ." I hated staying after school because it was a beautiful spring day, the kind that would "sprout leaves on a post."

I always got my clothes dirty. Some mothers told their daughters not to play with "that Williams girl" because I didn't keep clean. I didn't want to play with them anyway. When they came out to recess, they wore pretty sunbonnets and little white gloves. I wanted to play baseball with the boys. I was a good player and was sure to be chosen for a team.

In high school I played football with the "big boys." We played in a nearby cow pasture because it was the only place around that had a soft turf. I was accepted as a player by all except Frank Wykowski who picked on me. Somehow he always managed to shove me into a "cow pie." I was embarrassed, but I had sense enough to know that if I made an issue of it, I wouldn't get to play.

I grew up independent as a bird. I loved my parents, but our home life was unstable. Dad gradually began drinking, and the fact that Mother was 12 years older than Dad didn't help any either. I wanted a place where I could be alone. Once I discovered a space in the at-

My 1910 high school class. From left: Harvey Mooney, myself, Gladys Hastings, Laura Klaurtter, Bessie Spaur, General Million, Elmer Baum, Harold Hayward, Prof. Ryan, Maude Lapsley, Clarence Jeffries, Opal Stanger, Edwin Mahon, and Lola Fulton.

tic above our main room that looked like it had possibilities. If I could find a board to make a floor, I thought it could be my solitary place.

It happened one day, near the grain elevators, that I saw a hardwood board exactly the size I wanted. It was lying by the tracks where the freight cars were loaded. One edge had a tongue and the other a groove. It was a board that joined with others to close off the doorway of a freight car to hold the grain inside. I was so obsessed with the idea of solitude that it never occurred to me that I shouldn't take it. To keep from marring it, I carried the heavy board all the way home, instead of dragging it.

I took it upstairs, stood on a chair and began to maneuver it through the attic hole. It was all I could do to place it across the two-by-fours and pull myself up onto it. It was hard and uncomfortable. There was not enough room to move, and it was much too hot up there. My efforts had failed. It seemed I would never have a place to be alone.

When I went from Eugene, Oregon, to Cooksville at the age of 87 for its centennial celebration in July of 1982, I was surprised to learn that the board was still in the attic. The Garfield Avenue building had been somewhat remodeled inside, and someone lived there. The owner asked me about the board and wanted to know how I got it up there; he had been trying to get it down. I told him that I didn't know. When I did it, I was just "that Williams girl," and she did anything she set her mind to.

CHAPTER SIX

Friendly Contacts

"Thou preparest a table before me . . ."
—Psalm 23:5 (KJV)

While I lacked communication and warmth at home, a few friends and neighbors filled in for me.

Mrs. Felkamp, a Polish woman, lived in Fletcher. It was her son who married my Aunt Maggie. Mrs. Felkamp knew I liked her homemade bread and invited me to come every Thursday at the time it came out of the oven. I rode five miles on my bicycle to get a piece.

She would hand it to me dripping with butter, then pat me on the head and, in her Polish accent, say: "Poor kid." For a long time, I didn't know why she said it, but it was because she knew my mother had no oven at the telephone office in which to bake bread. Mrs. Felkamp became a dear friend.

I often ate at the Burbanks. They had left their farm to a son and moved into Cooksville. It was their custom to set an extra place at their table in case anyone dropped in, and I did. Their hospitality convinced me that they cared, and I enjoyed visiting with them because they had interesting things to say.

There was another place I liked to eat and the food was always good. All of Cooksville would join the annual Sunday School picnic on the Mackinaw River. It was a five-mile trip to a lovely shady spot, and we rode there on farm wagons pulled by the steam traction engines that powered the threshers. Benches from the church were used for seats. The young people jumped off and on the wagons, teasing one another, and, when they could get away with it, they snatched morsels from the food baskets.

I might have grown up without any refinement, but two fine women were especially concerned about me. I call them my "angels." One was Mrs. Scott, the other, Mrs. Dunlevy.

Early in life I learned to listen, so I knew a lot of things about Mrs. Henrietta Scott before I met her. She was a highly respected and talented school teacher. She often filled in as town clerk. She taught a women's Bible class, and she influenced the lives of many young people in Blue Mound Township. She had a crippled foot, of which I could never catch a glimpse because of her flowing skirts, though, I admit, I tried.

The Scotts had moved to town from their farm in Fletcher. It is now an historical landmark. James and his wife, Henrietta Scott, raised four successful children there. Walter Dill Scott was president of Northwest University, and John A. Scott was dean and professor of Greek at the same institution. One daughter was my school teacher and another daughter became a minister's wife.

My contact with Mrs. Scott came when her granddaughter finished high school and went to Europe, leaving her bicycle behind. Mrs. Scott gave it to me. It was too big, and Dad put blocks on the pedals so I could ride it.

She also knew a lot about me. Everyday I had to go past the Scott's house on my bicycle to get milk. The milk container was a Karo syrup bucket hung on the handlebars. I usually rode on the boardwalk, which was a forbidden place to cyclists. The sight of me whizzing by like a boy with no hands on the handlebars indicated something about my character to Mrs. Scott. Also, when I got a five-dollar fine for riding on the walk, she knew about it because it was recorded by the town clerk. After a while, the arresting officer left me alone because he knew the road was full of ruts.

I was contrary. If someone wanted me to say yes, I said no. If they wanted me to say no, I answered yes, and Mrs. Scott knew that. But, she also knew how to get what she wanted from me by using reverse psychology.

There came a time when I noticed she was out in her yard every time I went for milk. At first, she merely spoke to me, then she got me to stop. Finally, she had me in her house.

It was her aim to interest me in books. She had a lovely library. I couldn't read yet, so she showed me pictures and told me about exotic places.

"My" Henrietta Scott. (Courtesy of Laurel Quaid)

Once I reached out to take a book and, to my surprise, she pulled it back.

"No, your hands are too dirty," she said. Her words hit me like
a blow on the head. I looked at my hands, then quickly looked away.
I thought of the trouble it was to wash them—getting water from
the pump, heating it on the kerosene burner, scrubbing at the wash-
stand, emptying the water. In no time, they would be dirty again.

"If I let you hold my books, I will have to wrap them in paper to keep them clean," Mrs. Scott said.

Silently, I thought: "Oh, no, you won't. You won't have to wrap them for me!"

Then and there, I determined to have clean hands every time I went by Mrs. Scott's. Clean hands became the key to fascinating books. I began to feel that I should see Mrs. Scott regularly. Little did I know she had plans. By a mysterious process, she taught me to read. Next, she would leave me alone with a book to study. When she came back, she would ask questions to see if I had skipped anything. I tried very hard to learn because I hated to be wrong. A time came when I was permitted to take books home; I felt great accomplishment.

I liked to read more than anything. My favorite place was on a limb of the old cherry tree on the back of the lot where the hotel had burned. One beautiful spring morning, when the tree was full of blossoms, I climbed the twisted trunk and pulled myself up to my perch. I was sitting there reading when a lady I didn't know came and spoke to me in a soft voice. I looked down. She was charming and wore a Sunday dress. I realized it was Sunday morning.

She asked me in an irresistible manner if I would go with her to church. At that time, I rarely went, but I didn't say no. I slid down out of the tree and went with her. To cooperate was totally out of character.

The church was an old frame building with a steeple bell. Inside, we sat on a pew near the back. It was the woman's husband, Reverend O. M. Dunlevy, who preached. I was as much impressed by Mrs. Dunlevy's sweet, pleasant countenance as I was by his sermon. I kept looking up at her face hoping she wouldn't notice.

I went to church regularly after that and eventually received Jesus Christ as my personal savior. But it was a long time before I accepted Him as Lord and spiritual growth began. It took a crisis during my marriage to bring me to that.

These two ladies, Mrs. Scott and Mrs. Dunlevy, filled a great void in my life. Mrs. Scott, through her library, opened the world to me, and Mrs. Dunlevy, by taking me to church, opened heaven to me.

The kindnesses of all of these dear people kept me from growing up like a wild prairie flower. Each friendly contact made a special contribution to my life.

CHAPTER SEVEN

The "Velie 40"

"In all labor there is profit . . ."
—Proverbs 14:23 (KJV)

The Velie "40", 1910.

It was 1910. Three beautiful automobiles were being unloaded at the Cooksville frieght depot, and a large crowd had gathered to see them. They were ordered by telephone company officials who were tired of riding in buggies. They ordered expensive cars rather than the Fords the ordinary farmers purchased. The cars were Velie 40's shipped out of Moline. Each cost $1,800 FOB. It took several men to lift each of them from the frieght car to the platform, and an anxious crowd watched every move.

As Dad moved in closer, I had to keep moving to stay beside him. It wasn't long before he was running his hand over one of the automobiles. He walked around it, looked inside, and finally sat in the driver's seat. He was observed by envious onlookers who soon began cheering him. He smiled and waved like a candidate for a political office. A few decided to give the car a shove and others joined. As they pushed, Dad steered the Velie onto the ball park over by the school grounds. There they stopped. But, Dad wasn't through. He wanted to really drive the car.

He looked across the crowd and took command of some of the livelier instigators. Sending them for water, gas, and oil, he handed the driver's manual to me to read to him so he could figure out the mechanics before they got back. When everything was readied, Dad started the engine. He drove several times around the park, and the crowd went wild. He waved and smiled to accomodate them. Had Dad not worked for the men who purchased the Velies, he would not have been so bold. Showing off was not the greatest thing on his mind either; he was making plans. Dad enjoyed the mechanics of the Velies so much that he announced he was going to open a garage in Cooksville for automobile repair. There were no garages for several miles.

Dad wasted no time. He looked the town over for a suitable building, but there wasn't one. He had to build. He was able to purchase the land across from the telephone building, and because new lumber was too expensive, he acquired used lumber. The Union Church out in the country was abandoned. Dad bought it for a reasonable price and tore it down. There were large combs of honey in its walls, and the money from the sales helped buy building materials.

Dad also saved an old dilapidated pump organ from the church which he stored in a building behind the telephone office. The mice had eaten the bellows and the sound was poor, but all the keys were there. By this time in my life, I was ready to practice. I borrowed music from the church and tried my best. I progressed to a degree of proficiency and was asked to play at church. That didn't mean I was good. It meant there was no one else who could do it better.

I spent a lot of time alone in the storage room. Besides playing the organ, I watched the mice that slipped out of hiding to eat the hazel nuts that were spread out on the floor to dry. How could creatures so small crack such hard shells? One day I realized that in that dark and dusty place I had found the solitude I had looked for so long.

When it was time to build the garage, Dad included me in the planning. (From the moment I was born I was bonded to my dad. As I grew, I chose to be with him. When I was old enough, I worked beside him like a son.) We had two sections—one for automobiles and the other for bicycle sales and repairs. The bicycle shop was mine. I did my own bicycle repairs, so it was something I could handle.

For a while business was slow, but that didn't matter because Dad still worked for the telephone company and I was in high school. When I was not in school, I joined the harvesters.

I liked the work, not only for the money, but also for the tasty dinners. I knew when a meal was ready before the noon whistle blew, because I watched for the women to cover the food with cloths to keep off the flies.

I went along to eat with the men. The women, wearing long calico aprons, lifted the covers and we sat down. There was fried chicken, mashed potatoes, gravy, green beans with bacon, corn, homemade breads, plenty of butter and apple pie. There was lemonade and coffee.

The wives did not welcome me eating with their menfolk. They stared, whispered and shook their heads at one another. They succeeded in making me feel uncomfortable, but I knew I had worked the same as the men. I could throw bundles of oats into the thresher and pitch hay just as fast. I felt justified.

When I finished high school, there was enough work for me in the garage with Dad.

Early cars lacked headlights, so we added bicycle carbide lamps until the factories began to put on headlights. They were fueled by a presto tank that sat on the running board. The tank had a tendency to bounce off on rough roads so we secured it with a metal strap. I made the straps. I fired the forge, heated the metal bar, laid it on the anvil and beat it flat.

We had to make license plates for new cars, too. Numbers had to be pounded into the metal plate. Inexperienced drivers also made work for us because they sometimes thought a car knew where to go like the horse did. They often ended in the ditch. It was my job to get the car out and to the garage. It took ingenuity because we had no wrecker.

Dad's and my garage.

Our method of operation (1915). The telephone building is on the right. I am driving the car which Mother and I drove to Kentucky.

Waiting for me.

I remembered that Fred Wykowski owned a trailer for hauling irrigation pipes. I thought it would hold a car. I figured I could use it to bring in the wrecks.

Dad owned an International Harvester automobile which I learned to drive when I was 16. I drove it out to Wykowski's and got permission to use the trailer. I hooked it behind Dad's car with a heavy chain.

Though the whole rig was oversize, I drove it through town. As many times as I did this, I was never stopped. It seemed that whenever Dick Williams's daughter stretched the law, it was overlooked by the authorities. They never knew what to do with me.

It was at the scene of the first wreck that I realized I hadn't thought things through. I hadn't brought anyone to help me. I stood there and laughed. I looked around. There was just me and the car, and I knew the car couldn't give any help. There was a jack. With it, I could go at the job one end at a time.

I jacked up one part and pushed and shoved until one end of the car was on the trailer. Then I jacked up the other end and went at it again, pushing and shoving, until I had the whole wreck on the outfit. Fortunately, the trailer was low to the ground or I could

Our home after the telephone company employment.

Some members of the Cooksville business district. The two ladies, Loretta Guy and Mary Currings, with Sonny Currings, ran the hardware store. Dad and I ran Dick's Garage.

The Cooksville Hardware.

Cooksville, Illinois—1909.

not have managed. I could have hurt myself, but, whatever it took, I wanted to please Dad. I had heard that the Good Lord looks out for fools and children, and I figured I must have had double indemnity. I loaded the automobile by strength and awkwardness.

Of all the jobs Dad had, he was most content as an auto mechanic. The work came naturally to him, and it did to me. Whatever he could do, I could do. Soon, customers preferred my work for carburetors, valve settings, vibrators and adjusting.

Dad turned one job over to me completely. He had bought a steam vulcanizer. It blew up every time he used it, so he left tire repair to me.

Finally, Dad gave up his employment with the telephone company. People couldn't understand why he would give up a good job that paid $75 a month and a place to live just to run a garage. But he was content as a mechanic. He had discovered the workings of a beautiful automobile called a Velie 40 and it made him want to be a mechanic. We moved into a nice little house on Main Street. It was a real change for us. Mother became a full-time housewife, and I got a room of my own. That meant a lot to me. I was 18 and courting age.

CHAPTER EIGHT

Courtship and Marriage

"Doth not wisdom cry? And understanding put forth her voice?"
—Proverbs 8:1 (KJV)

There were several young men who were attracted to me, but I had not been taught how to choose a life mate.

Ed Small came to church from Colfax with two gentlemen who were courting two girlfriends of mine. It seemed it was more intriguing to court girls six miles away from home.

Because Ed had no one to be with, my parents allowed me to visit with him. Besides, I was attracted to him. He was big and tall with thick, dark, wavy hair, and had a kind face.

Courting went slowly because the fellows just came every other Sunday. There were no buggy rides; the horse had to rest for the trip home. It was unhitched and allowed to graze. We walked in the churchyard in the summertime or sat on the steps. When winter came, we huddled around the stove inside.

It was winter when Ed and I got "moonstruck." We made a mistake not to talk about ourselves; our likes and dislikes; our different ways. Instead we "smooched." I assumed he was like the sons of other farmers, a hard worker and able to make a living. In turn, he took it for granted that I was the domestic type.

Ed and I were as opposite as could be. He was the domestic—even his mother's "daughter." Due to a foot injury when a steam radiator fell on him in high school, he was unable to do farm work. His mother let her help go and hired him to do her housework. I had never washed a dish, let alone done housework—I was my father's "son." It was trouble ahead, if we married.

39

After high school, Ed had a job teaching in the Colfax grade school. Consequently, he had some experience outside of the house, but he could never take on heavy work.

We courted for a year. If he asked me to marry him, I don't remember. We married in the midst of a tragedy, and I think Ed was pushed into it. For myself, I was too broken-hearted to be responsible for what I did. Whatever was suggested, I followed it.

One day while I was working with Dad, I said that I thought it would be kind of nice to get married. It was later in the day that he thought back on what I had said. He believed it was my way of telling him I planned to marry Ed. But Ed had not asked me.

Dad got excited. He had two friends who always welcomed an excuse to have a drink, and they got together that night to celebrate. The two men got so drunk they couldn't go home. Dad took them to the Green Hotel which was then owned by my Aunt Mattie. Aunt Maggie ran the hotel for Aunt Mattie, and she showed Dad where to put his friends.

When he had put them each into a bed, he went to the stairs to go down. It was a narrow, dark stairwell, and Dad missed his footing on the top step. He fell head first to the bottom and broke his neck. At that time, a broken neck was fatal.

Mother and I were notified, and so was Cooksville's Dr. Mahon. Dad was taken to the hospital in Bloomington in an automobile with collapsible seats, because there was no ambulance.

Weeping all the way, I rode along the 25 miles. I knew my dear daddy, who had been my friend and partner all my life, was dying.

I was shocked beyond my senses. He was brought home, where I sat for ten days and never left his side. He died on November 28, 1914. The funeral was the largest ever in the area because my dad was so well-known.

(It was the next year that the Village Board of Cooksville passed a resolution stating that liquor disturbed the peace and quiet of the town, and the shipping of liquor was banned. The resolution came too late for Dad.)

Stunned and in agony from my loss, my whole being hurt. I couldn't face the fact that Dad was gone. Ed thoughtfully came to be there if I needed him, but it was useless. I didn't notice him. I was out of reality.

I had nothing to do with the planning of my wedding. In that time, when there was no psychiatric help, people did whatever they could think of to snap someone back to reality. My concerned relatives did that for me. They, with Mother, believing that Ed and I were engaged, planned our wedding. Ed didn't have a chance. He cared about me, and he didn't back out—possibly because he thought it would add to my emotional sickness, if he did. I probably thought he had agreed with my relatives that he wanted to marry me. I have never recalled a time when he asked me. I did like him. This is the best I can explain what happened to us.

Twenty-two days after Dad's death, we were married. It was Ed's birthday December 19. It was a simple, inexpensive ceremony. I wore a blue poplin dress I already had. A few guests came from the telephone company, the railroad, neighboring towns and farms. Sixteen people attended the wedding and reception at our home.

When it was over, Ed and I walked to the depot and took the five o'clock train to Colfax. He had rented a house there, and I had bought some furniture.

CHAPTER NINE

Mother, My Mother

". . . Let her own works praise her in the gates."
—Proverbs 31:31 (KJV)

Ed and I started housekeeping. We had no income and had to depend on his parents for food. They always put up more than was needed and didn't mind sharing, but it was a tense situation for me. I hated being dependent on Ed's folks. Added to that, I heard a rumor that his mother had picked out someone she wanted him to marry. It wasn't me. As far as I was concerned, we had to get away from there, and we needed to get work. Mother wanted us to come back to Cooksville. The garage closed when Dad died and Mother knew it could be our income. She moved into the George Swinehart house with two stories and suggested that we move in with her and run the garage. We went back to Cooksville.

It was February 1915. Customers started coming right away. However, Ed was by no means a mechanic and people preferred me to do their work. The first time Ed worked on someone's car, the owner never let him touch it again. If I was out of the garage and a customer came in, Ed was asked, "Is Grace here?" That was hard to take. He believed that, as a man he should be head of the business, but the customers thought I was.

Ed was not the only one at fault. I couldn't manage housekeeping. For myself, I would have rather been in the garage. Ed would probably have rather been in the house.

Fear took hold of me when I learned we were going to have a child. I had never been around infants. Morning sickness hit me hard. I missed my Dad. He had always been my encouragement. Ed's ef-

I try to fill my new role (1915).

forts didn't help, and I became depressed. I thought there was no one to turn to. Then I discovered Mother. I hadn't known her as well as I knew Dad.

She observed my depression. No doubt she recalled her own pregnancy 20 years before, the depression she felt, the bare, desolate land she looked at from her window in Merna. She probably recalled crawling under the table to shut out the world.

She knew I needed change. One day she announced that she was planning a trip for the two of us to go to my Grandmother Mills's house in Somerset. That got my attention when nothing else did.

When I was small, we had gone to my Grandmother Mills's several times because the Illinois Central Railroad offered special rates to drum up business. That was when I met more cousins and saw the old mill on Pittman's Creek. I also enjoyed the train ride. I knew this trip with Mother would be a change and maybe even restful.

To my surprise, Mother said she wanted us to go by automobile. She wanted us to visit old friends she could not see if we went by train. Ed encouraged us, so we packed ourselves into Dad's old International Harvester. I did the driving since Mother didn't know how, and we set off for Somerset.

It was July. The sun was shining when we started and we left the car top down. Along the way it began to rain. Because it took several people to put the top up, we got wet. I watched Mother. With the rain falling on her, she sat straight in her seat and looked ahead as if the sun were shining. She never once complained.

Our way was unmapped. There were no interstate highways, and we had to pioneer our trail over rutted farm roads. To find our way, we followed telephone lines. Had we not worked for the telephone company, we probably would not have known that the poles with cross arms led to towns, and the ones with brackets went to and from farm houses. Occasionally, we got onto a smooth road made by linemen. The perspiration poured off me as I worked to steer the car over the rough places. There was no such thing as power steering.

We were challenged often by deep mud through which the car refused to move. We took off our shoes, waded in and pushed until the wheels were free. When we came to a creek, we cleaned our feet.

Once we came to a crossroad near a farm. The ground was sloppy and wet. A young boy approached us and urged us to take a different direction. "If you get stuck, I can get you out," he offered. It was evident that he wanted us to get stuck so we would have to pay him to get us out. We went the other way without mishap.

We stayed at night with Mother's friends who were glad to see us, and people were amazed by our grit. We were taking a 500-mile trip and most of it was through mud. One man at a gas station encouraged us, "If you can make it to Scottsburg, you will make it to Kentucky."

Through Indiana, we crossed the Ohio River by ferry. Between the Ohio and Scottsburg, the way was so muddy we honestly thought we couldn't make it. The mud was as high as the wheel hubs.

We looked it over, then, we took off our shoes and got out of the car to test the road. We decided it would support the car and began pushing with me leaning in to steer. With great effort, we eventually made it through.

At last, we arrived in Kentucky and went on to Somerset. I pumped up tires five times on the trip, and all in all, we were too exhausted to visit. We went to bed immediately when we reached Grandma Mills's. One way or another, I was getting a change.

The South was beautiful. We went first to relatives whose house was on top of a green, wooded hill. We were busy visiting when we heard the frantic voices of the children who had been playing around the car. We hurried out and saw that one of the boys had let the brake loose. The car started down the hill. Several of them joined to stop it before it rolled into the springhouse below.

There was one place Mother went alone. That was to the graveyard behind Soules Chapel. There was something special about visiting the place where Grandpa and other members of our family were buried.

The road that led to the graveyard was not really a road, but a creek bed of great, flat rocks. It was too rough for me in my condition, but Mother was determined. She got an old, worn mare that was the only horse left on the place and borrowed a neighbor's mule. She hitched them to the running gear of a dilapidated, mud-covered farm wagon. She found a split-hickory-bottom chair and placed it precariously on the wagon bed, climbed in, and sat on it. She was neatly dressed, clean, hatted, and dignified as she took up the reins.

I watched her drive down the creek bed as if she were driving a matched team at the county fair. That was Mother!

For all of the effort it took to get to Somerset, we stayed only a week. We returned to Cooksville over the same muddy route. My depression was gone.

Home again, I went back to work in the garage. There was much to do. Even when I was fully expanded around the middle. there were occasions when I had to go out and haul in a wrecked car.

Baby Edna Eileen arrived in January, and a few days afterward I went back to work. Mother took care of Edna (later called Eileen) so I could help Ed make a living. Mother was needed.

When I thought back on her, I remembered that she learned to cope with every situation. She could make do with what she had. When we moved from the telephone office to the house on Main Street, we no longer had the town pump behind our house. Mother was used to having water close at hand and was determined she would have it. She took several tin cans and put them together to make a drain pipe and used halves of cans cut the long way to make a gutter at the edge of the roof. When it rained, the water ran off into the gutter and down into a barrel. There was plenty of water for laundry, baths and cleaning. Mother also adjusted to very simple housedresses and rough shoes, so different from the lovely clothes she wore in Kentucky. Her youthful face that once attracted suitors years ago was lined and her auburn hair had turned to gray. She accepted the fact that she could not have youth forever.

It was at this time in life that I discovered my mother, my precious mother.

CHAPTER TEN

Chauffeuring, Bloomington and Babies

*"Keep thy heart with all diligence, for out of it
are the issues of life."*
— *Proverbs 4:23 (KJV)*

In the early 1900s women were expected to stay at home. But they were gradually gaining freedom. At age 21, I was one of the few automobile drivers in Cooksville. As more men owned cars, they came to me to teach them to drive. I taught a few women to drive too, because their husbands wouldn't teach them.

One man I taught was John Golden, a prominent citizen of Cooksville. During World War I, he was a mule buyer for the Army. After traveling by horseback day after day to the corrals, he realized how slow it was and bought a car. He asked me to teach him how to drive.

That wasn't easy. He sat behind the steering wheel and started the engine. I assumed he was going to steer the car. But I soon learned that, as a driving instructor, I couldn't assume anything. Driving a car was a whole new concept for John. When the car went forward, he just let go in the same way he would have given a horse its head. Before I could do anything, the car hit the watering trough.

John gave up learning right then. I chauffeured him the rest of the day so he could look at mules. The next day he didn't want to take any more chances, and I had to chauffeur him the rest of the summer. The following year, he had his confidence back and learned to drive.

Travel by horseback was becoming less popular. Salesmen who came in on the train wanted to do their routes by car rather than rent livery horses. I saw the opportunity to chauffeur using Dad's old International Harvester touring car and decided to get a license.

I wrote to Springfield, Illinois, and arranged for a local driving test. It amused me to find that the examiner appointed to me was a man I had taught to drive. Of course I passed the test. I became the first female chauffeur in Illinois outside the city of Chicago.

I chauffeured day and night. If there was an extra car needed for a wedding or funeral, I was called. I took drunks to their homes after dark. As long as I got ten cents a mile, it didn't matter to me who my passengers were. I earned enough money the first year to buy a used Model A Ford.

The day our second child was born, I chauffeured a salesman on his route to five farms. Our son, Richard Joseph, was born at nine o'clock that night. After two weeks, I was on the road again, and Mother had another grandchild to care for.

I realized that my chauffeuring left Ed alone in the garage, but I was making badly needed money. He tried to keep the garage going, but eventually we had to close it.

It pleased us that it did not take long for Ed to get a good job. Snow and Palmer Dairy Products in Bloomington had changed from horsedrawn wagons to motorized vehicles and needed mechanics. Good ones were hard to find, and, by this time, Ed knew more than most.

We moved to Bloomington and took Mother with us. We rented a house that needed improvements and fixed it up into an attractive place. The landlord promptly raised the rent. We couldn't afford to pay what he wanted, so we had to move again.

Houses that suited us were too expensive. The only one we could find was in a segregated part of town. We didn't belong there and may not have been wanted, either. But we moved in and stayed many years. That house at 1002 East Empire became our home.

For the first time, Ed's income made it possible for me to stay with our children.

When our third child was born, I wanted Ed to take me to the hospital, but he couldn't get off work. So I took a taxi. The first two babies had been born at home, and the hospital was a new ex-

We purchased 1002 E. Empire Street in 1925. (Courtesy of Hazel Arbuckle)

perience. I didn't like it because no one knew me in Bloomington the way they did in Cooksville. I felt alone.

At the end of the day, when Ed came to see me and our new daughter, I was overjoyed to see him. We named the baby Elizabeth Adrid.

Again, when another child was due I counted on Ed to take me to the hospital. But the baby came in the daytime and he said he needed to sleep. While he slept, I took a taxi.

The fourth child was also a girl. When Ed came to see us after work, he surprised me by announcing, "Her name is Hazel Virginia." In wonder, I drew a slow, deep breath. Then, I learned that two young women who worked at the plant with Ed were Hazel and Virginia. I was filled with a jealous hurt.

We had one more child nine years later, a boy. He was stillborn, and we buried him in the Pleasant Hill Cemetery in McLean County July 11, 1931. We didn't name him, but we often spoke of him as "Timmie Tom Small."

Mother began to work out of the home doing housework after Hazel was born, and Ed's and my four children got my full attention.

CHAPTER ELEVEN

My Business is Children

"This also I saw, that it was from the hand of God."
—Ecclesiastes 2:24 (KJV)

The years had made a drastic change in my life. As a child, I had never thought of having a home and family. Now, I was deeply involved in rearing four children.

On Sundays I took them to church while Ed was asleep. Although he rarely took part in our activities, he did take us to see his parents in Colfax after the service. It was a hard trip for me. Cars went slowly then, and the 30 miles was much too far with four children. I tried to keep them entertained, but the bare monotonous landscape offered no reprieve. Finally, when they caught sight of the water tower on Grandpa Small's farm, there were shouts of joy. That to me was a sign of impending relief from the confinement of the car.

The end of one thing was the beginning of another, however. Ed's mother always found fault with the children's clothes. One had a string hanging, or one had a faded sock; one girl's dress was too long or hung crooked. I knew I had done the best I could with what I had, but I was very uncomfortable in her presence, partly because I knew I was not her choice for Ed's wife. I was glad when the visit was over. The children were tired on the way home and usually fell asleep. Thankful it was over, I relaxed on the way back.

While Ed slept during the day, I had to find ways to keep the children quiet. It took a lot of ingenuity as we didn't have money for toys and amusements. I often got cabin fever being cooped up with them.

One day an idea came to me to build a doll house. With the

These are the four Smalls in Bloomington (1922).

children watching close by, I laid out the plans and explained the steps in building.

The peak of the roof was 36 inches high. There were two stories and partitions to divide the rooms. Each room had finished ceilings and walls, and the doors and windows opened. The structure was extraordinary.

Some people in Bloomington who saw it wanted to buy it, so it was sold. The buyers used it as part of a Christmas display in their home adding snow on the roof and tiny lights on a Christmas tree inside. A picture of it was published on the front page of the local newspaper.

My children enjoyed the building activity so much that I made two more houses. While all of the houses were wired for electricity,

One of the three doll houses.

the second one had lights and switches in every room. The back part of the roof was hinged to open so the switches could be reached. One house had castors and my children rode it around. I finally gave it to a children's institution to save it from falling apart.

The owner of the Green Mill Cafe in Bloomington saw pictures of my first dollhouse and hired me to build a small windmill for the window of his restaurant. I wired it for electricity so the sails would turn, and an axle connection below allowed it to pivot in any direction. The project provided extra money for our family.

Even though it was my father who taught me to build, I believe my talent for it came from my mother's side of the family. When I visited Yorkshire, England, in 1964, I studied my family history and learned that in the 1800s, when most men in the area worked in the coal mines, her ancestors were skilled cabinet makers. It is no wonder building came natural to me.

I continued to enjoy carpentry. After the children were grown,

The house I built in Bloomington—how it looks today.

I built a house. A daughter and son-in-law were living with us while looking for a house. We were crowded and I solved the problem by building one for them on our lot. I took a loan and bought used lumber. The house is now a pretty little place in Bloomington. It is nicely painted and someone has added a porch.

I didn't just entertain my own children. Our yard was a gathering place for the neighborhood youngsters. Because I had a car, I chauffeured my children to school. Their friends rode too. It was common to see my Model A Ford full of wiggling pupils, some black and some white. They rode inside the car and on the running board. Whatever made them happy made me happy.

One day I got myself into trouble. We had started for school when the Goodyear blimp floated over us. It was something none of us had seen. It drifted toward the airport and I knew it would anchor there. The children and I were eager, so I drove to the airport. We absorbed the sight of the blimp anchoring. Then I told the children we must get them back to school.

We were late, and I was more than shocked when we arrived. The school authorities were waiting on the walk for us. The children were sent inside and, in short order, I was scolded and informed that "the children should have been brought to school on time!"

Parents, notified that their children were missing, showed up shouting: "It was not your place to make such a decision." "You had no right to take our children to the airport without our permission." I was terribly embarrassed to be confronted by my neighbors, but they were right and I apologized.

I realized my curiosity hadn't changed much through the years. The reprimand reminded me of the incident with Bill Lake and his racehorse, Tanglefoot. In both cases, I meant no harm and each event held a tongue-lashing for me. I consoled myself again with the thought that people in Bloomington didn't know me like those in Cooksville did.

The children were my business. One by one, they grew to adulthood and went their ways.

CHAPTER TWELVE

My Desperate Effort

"Fearfulness and trembling are come over me,
and horror hath overwhelmed me."
—*Psalm 55:5*

After the children were gone, I hoped Ed would take some interest in going to church and having friends. But the more I tried to make it come about, the more he pulled away. Because he worked nights, we seldom saw each other. Finally, it became evident that we had grown apart and he didn't care. The reality hurt me to the core.

In desperation, I turned to the Lord. Though I was a Christian, I didn't know the Lord as a person. I began to study the Bible intently. The Lord became real to me, and the fellowship exceeded any experience I had ever had.

I was a member of the Presbyterian Church in Bloomington and was asked to teach a class of young servicemen. Though I felt I should have had more education for the job, I knew the Lord would help me present the Bible.

The needs of the young men were grave. It was always on my mind that they might go into battle and not return. Therefore, I was all the more diligent in my study in order to pass on truth. The class ended when the men shipped out.

I was stunned the day Ed announced he wanted a divorce. I was further shocked when he said he was in love with a friend of one of our daughters. I tried to get him to see what he was doing, but he could not hear.

Because I was stubborn, I tried a method I hoped would get his

Some of my young service men (1941). Do you know any of them?

attention. I recalled the phrase, "Absence makes the heart grow fonder," and decided to just sort of disappear. If Ed cared, I reasoned, he would try to find me. I knew a place to go.

I had a desire to go to Biloxi, Mississippi, to see my grandson Jimmy on his fifth birthday. He had lived near us and had recently moved away; I missed him. I knew a surprise visit would make us both happy, and his unconditional love would be a balm for my wounded spirit. Without seeking the Lord's will, I set my mind to go.

There was one big problem. I didn't have bus money for the trip. We had $20 that came from the sale of a second car, but it was earmarked for replacing the worn living room rug. In any event, it was not enough.

It flashed through my mind that I could hitchhike. It was a common thing for young people to hitchhike the ten miles between Bloomington and the Civilian Conservation Corps camp to skate. And I had earlier gone hiking a few times to Anchor 20 miles away to escape "cabin fever."

It was an irrational idea, however, as I would put myself in jeopardy. My destination was 1,000 miles away. It was winter, not summer, and my age was 46. Common sense never entered into my decision—I was desperate to win Ed back.

I packed light and left behind the impression that I was going to visit Henry and Ova Harms in Anchor. No questions were asked.

It was January 28 and it was snowing. I tightly clutched the handle of my little suitcase as I walked to the edge of town to catch my first ride.

My heavy tweed coat shut out the wind, but the blowing snow stung my face. The tailored felt hat I wore did not cover my ears. I was cold and uncomfortable.

I took the first ride offered me without thinking to ask where the driver was going. The man lived nearby and took me two miles. That was not progress.

I got out, tucked my head into the wind, and struck out again. I walked until I had blisters.

I got a few short rides. The last one of the day took me 150 miles. I was very cold and tense when I got into the car with a middle-aged man. I held tightly to a rolled up newspaper that I carried to put on the floor in case my shoes were dirty.

The driver began talking and revealed that his wife had died recently. He seemed unusually nervous. I thought it was because of his sorrow, but when I began to thaw out, I loosened my grip on the newspaper and pressed it flat on my lap. The man sighed a sigh of relief. He thought I was concealing a gun.

My total distance for the first day was about 250 miles. I thought it a good start toward my goal. I stayed overnight in a rooming house in Anna, Illinois. Fourteen young men lived there who worked at a nearby Army ordnance plant. There were no vacancies, but the woman proprietor let me in. She made up a couch and put an enclosure around it. She said there would be no charge.

The woman was extraordinarily kind. When she learned that I had blisters, she brought a basin of warm water and bathed my feet. She also warned me that the fresh black dye I had put on my shoes had stained my feet and could cause poisoning in the blisters. She cautioned me to watch them carefully.

The Lord was definitely watching over me, even when I did not acknowledge Him. I needed His help as I was not using good sense.

The next morning I got some advice. All the young men but one left for work. He and I ate breakfast together, and he gave me the "rules" for hitchhiking. But they came after he gave me a scolding for doing it.

"First," he said, "you never walk. Second, get away from the town to put your thumb up . . . go to the last stop light. Third, never accept short rides. Stay put. Wait for someone going a long way."

He left the house before I did, and I thought hard on what he had told me; I knew that he had given me good advice. When I left, I followed Rule Number One and started for the edge of town.

The air was bitter cold and I shivered. Hoarfrost covered the walk and my shoes left tracks as I walked along. In a while, I heard the rattling sound of an old car. It was the young man who had told me how to hitchhike. When he caught up with me, he stopped the car. The ordnance plant was in the other direction, and I knew he had come to give me a ride. He had gone to get gas.

He drove to a place where I could wait.

I was sorry that I didn't get his name; he gave me the most valuable help for all my years of hitchhiking.

My next driver did not dare to take me over the state line, so he left me on the Illinois border at Cairo. From there, a ride to Memphis ended the day. I stayed in a hotel like any other tourist and slept in a nice bed.

My faith was strong. I realized I had traveled many miles and was safe. No one had reason to miss me yet, but I hoped it would happen eventually.

I met a hitchhiker that day who was quite concerned for my safety. He gave me the address of his sister in Greenville, Alabama, and said I could stay overnight there. But I didn't plan to go that way. He urged me to stay at the Salvation Army or to ask the police to put me in jail overnight to keep me safe. He made every effort to make me see the seriousness of my undertaking. His genuine interest was more effective than a scolding would have been.

On the road the next morning, I felt confident enough to take a side trip with one of my rides. Two young men driving south wanted to see the Mississippi flood control system, and so did I. The sight was worth the 20-mile detour. But, when I stopped for the night I was in a very small town with no accommodations, no jail, and no all-night restaurant or bus depot.

Walking along the street, I felt the hair on the back of my neck rise as I passed a "spit and whittle club" in front of the gas station. I had expected stares, but not the disgusting leers these men gave me. Not far beyond them was a gang of rowdy, shouting people. It was getting dark and I was apprehensive about going further. My confidence of the morning left me. I knocked at the door of a lighted house nearby planning to beg for a place to stay.

The door opened and the light from the room shone on my face. The woman was frightened to see a stranger, perhaps a beggar, standing on her doorstep.

Desperate for words, she announced quickly, "I am a good Christian lady!" With that she shut the door. From the look on her face, I was already turning to go. I have since wondered whether or not she, as a Christian, knew about Christ's words on being hospitable to strangers.

From across the road, a small, dim light seemed to beckon me. I went over and presented myself at that door. What a contrast to the first house! A young couple with little to live on invited me in to the best they had. I was never treated better. They were truly "given to hospitality" as Romans 12:13 says.

They prepared supper over a cracked stove that stood on three legs. The meal, a "bit of cornpone" and a small sweet potato, was served to me in as gracious a manner as I have ever known.

They had a little daughter who showed her concern, too. She assisted while her mother bathed my feet. Sweet, loving words flowed from her mouth as she watched. The couple gave me their bed and made a place for themselves in the living room. I could hear their soft tones as they took turns reading scripture verses before they went to bed.

The morning light revealed a house in defiance of gravity. There were open spaces in the siding. Our worst chicken houses in Illinois were better built and gave more protection from the elements.

I noticed that the couple consistently showed one another kindness. Their love surpassed any I had observed in my entire life. It was overwhelming to me that they were willing to share themselves with a stranger.

I was near Biloxi where my daughter Eileen's husband was stationed. My next ride took me directly to her house. It was 10 a.m.

and I rang the doorbell. Jimmy opened the door. His scream of joy brought Eileen running, and she stared at me in disbelief. How did I get there?

She rightly disapproved when I told her, but I was welcomed and had a pleasant ten-day visit.

It refreshed my wounded spirit to visit some of the historical sites in the South. Eileen lived in an area with many antebellum mansions. Bright pink blossoms on huge bougainvillaea vines spread over large old worn-brick houses making them beautiful again. It was a diversion from the emptiness of my life in Bloomington.

In a great expanse of green lawn stood a huge live oak with limbs that spread far out like a hoop skirt. Spanish moss hung from its branches like tattered lace amid its shining leaves. Time, past and present, seemed to move with the breeze between its boughs. "The War Between the States," "The War to End All Wars," our country was at war. The old tree was a living witness to it all.

When I was ready to leave Biloxi, I counted my money. I had spent only $4.40. I was beginning to feel very confident that I could go where I pleased. I had always wanted to see and visit relatives and old friends in Kentucky. One friend was Mrs. Blackman, a former neighbor from Bloomington, who lived in Smyrna, Tennessee. I decided to see her first.

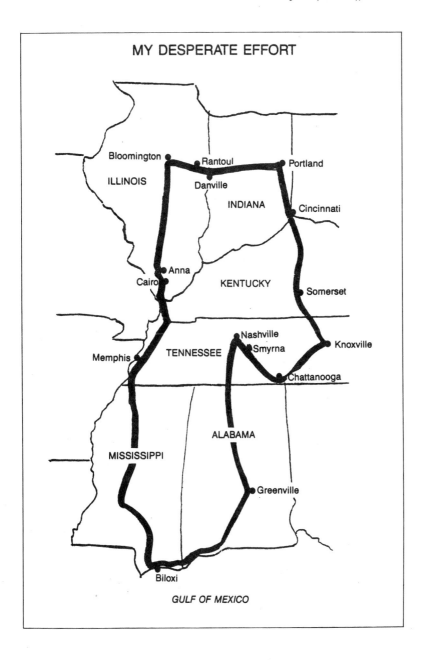

MY DESPERATE EFFORT

Bloomington
Rantoul
Portland
ILLINOIS
Danville
INDIANA
Cincinnati
Anna
Cairo
KENTUCKY
Somerset
Nashville
Smyrna
Knoxville
Memphis
TENNESSEE
Chattanooga
ALABAMA
MISSISSIPPI
Greenville
Biloxi
GULF OF MEXICO

CHAPTER THIRTEEN

The Way Home

"He knoweth the way that I take; when He has
tried me, I shall come forth as gold."
—Job 23:10 (KJV)

On the road again, I took a ride with an older man on his way to Alabama. Had I realized he had been drinking, I would not have gotten into the car. He was intently getting drunk to relax from his job of supervising the building of ordnance huts. He said he never drank on the job; he drank while on the road. He asked me to ride the whole day because he wanted someone who could grab the steering wheel if he passed out. I was not afraid, though I probably should have been. Driving with him stretched my money since he never stopped to eat. We did take one coffee break.

We talked a lot about local history, schools, religion, and American homes. We had many miles of silence, too, and I was very glad to get out at a junction near Andalusia, Alabama, where his next job was.

Now that I was in Alabama after all, I figured I could stay with the sister of the hitchhiker I had met earlier. I got a ride to Greenville and located the address. I learned the woman had moved to Detroit, so I had no free lodging that night. I knew I shouldn't spend much money and I began to search for an inexpensive place. I came upon a dreary rooming house that charged two dollars a night. I was skeptical but decided to stay anyway.

The place was so dirty I couldn't relax, let alone sleep. I was happy to leave in the morning, and I never took such a cheap place again.

Rides came slowly that day. The South definitely frowned on hitchhikers. By evening, two young men drove me to Athens and introduced me to a woman they knew who ran a hotel there. I got a good room and made up for the sleep I had lost the night before.

The laws governing hitchhiking were always close upon me. Once at the edge of a town, I was walking along an uphill curve. I was not ready to put out my thumb, but I was recognized as a hitchhiker by a truck driver. He came up behind me and stopped. The engine still running, he leaned over to the passenger side, reached his hand toward me and yelled, "Swing on, lady!"

There was no time to think. I took his hand and swung.

As the truck started he said, "The State Patrol is picking up every woman hitchhiker for miles around here because of the Army camps. They don't want any trouble. You don't need to think that you will be an exception."

He demanded that I tell him why I was trying to commit suicide. "That curve was a very dangerous place to catch a ride," he maintained. He took me far from the camp area so that I could get a ride in a car.

In contrast, my next ride was with a pretty young mother in a new car. She was on her way to see her mother and had her new tiny baby in a basket. We were glad for each other's company. It was refreshing when we stopped to eat in a restaurant and visit because it had been raining off and on for several days.

The young mother planned to stay over in Nashville, and my destination was not much further. I made the 14 miles in two rides and phoned the Blackmans' home. Though the family had just returned from Florida, they gave me a gracious welcome. They asked me to stay several days and, since I had no need to hurry, I said I would.

We started out that night getting caught up on the last few years. Early in the morning, a little black boy made the fires in the fireplaces. Mrs. Blackman fixed breakfast.

I told her that I had always wanted to see Lookout Mountain Park and planned to visit there on this trip. To my surprise, at breakfast I got anxious about going and left before our morning visit was over. It was an uncanny feeling that caused me to believe I should hurry. Mrs. Blackman did not understand and neither did I. I left the breakfast table in haste, packed my suitcase and grabbed my coat. I said a quick goodbye.

A lady waiting for a ride to work called to me. If I hurried, I could go to town with her. In town, I got a ride with four young men. I told them that I believed I should be in Chattanooga at the bottom of Lookout Mountain at the noon hour. They promised they could get me there on time. We arrived at the cable car at noon just before it ascended.

At the top the view was inspiring and I prayed as I walked around. Mostly I praised God for His goodness.

Later, a young man asked me if I had seen his friend. He was missing. They were both on the cable car when I went up. His absence caused a big commotion as park security searched for him. Late that afternoon, the young man was found resting on a ledge where he had fallen while taking a short cut. Pine needles had padded his fall. I knew that God had spared him. I don't know why I witnessed this event, but I know I became more aware about the power of God. I bought a postcard and sent it to Mrs. Blackman explaining what happened.

Next, I set out for Somerset, Kentucky, where my favorite cousin Ed Mills lived. Rides were hard to get, but in the afternoon three young men in a fairly nice Ford stopped for me. I took their offer, even though they were drinking. I would have enjoyed the beautiful Smokey Mountains more if they had not driven so fast and reckless. They were trying to scare me, but they scared themselves worse when the car nearly went over a cliff. They drove more sedately after that and made up for their wild antics by driving me directly to my cousin's place of work.

I was welcomed with open arms. Ed Mills and I hadn't seen each other for many years. When we were little, his dad layed a flat stick out in the pasture and put brown sugar on it. He would call us to come lick it up like little calves. It's things like that that made us close. Since it was not yet quitting time, Ed brought his car around and told me to drive it out to his farm and visit with his wife. We could return and pick him up later.

I stopped at a gas station to fill the tank. When I want to start the car again, I couldn't find the starter. My cousin had turned the car over to me with the engine running, and different makes of cars had different starters.

The young station attendant knew it was Ed's car and assumed I had stolen it. He hurriedly telephoned my cousin to tell him his car had been stolen by an old woman. Ed explained and I drove out to the farm.

While I visited in Somerset, the weather was below freezing, but there was warmth with my Kentucky kinfolk. I stayed ten days.

My cousin didn't want me to thumb so he bought me a bus ticket to Danville. He got angry with me when I tried to refuse it, so I accepted it reluctantly. We both knew I would cash it in and continue to hitchhike. I planned to see more friends before I got to Danville.

At the edge of town, I took the first ride offered me. That was a careless thing to do and not according to the hitchhiking rules given me.

It was a wreck of a car with two young men in it. I hoped I wouldn't be in the car long. It had bucket seats up front, and I had to sit on the hard space between because the boys were moving and the back seat was filled with their belongings.

The boys were full of fun and very nice. They took turns driving. We were getting near Portland, Indiana, where I had friends, when all at once the radiator spewed "cornmeal" all over the windshield. The driver put his head out the window so he could see to drive, and soon his face was covered with the stuff. A gas station was not far ahead. We stopped and they filled the radiator and gas tank, and the young man cleaned his face.

I got out and stretched. It was then the boys realized that I could use some padding on the place I was sitting. Even though I weighed only 125 pounds, I was very uncomfortable. They rumaged comically through their belongings to find a pillow so that the next few miles would be easier riding for me.

I had them let me out at the courthouse where the husband of my friend worked. It was near closing time when I arrived, and we were soon on our way to their home. They had a lovely farm, and a big meal was ready when we arrived. Mother and I had visited them on our trip to Somerset.

We had other friends, Ollie and Lola Whitehouse, who wanted to see me, too. I set out to get a ride to their place. I waited a long time in the cold evening air. A woman picked me up, but she took me the wrong way and I had to get out in the cold and start over. A soldier driving to Florida took me to a phone where I could call.

I had grown up with Ollie and Lola in Cooksville. He had become a preacher and had two churches because they lived near the time zone. He had a church on each side. I stayed several days and it was hard to leave.

It was snowing when they took me to a transcontinental highway where I could get started on my way home. It was asking a lot of this dear minister to put me out on the road in a blizzard, but they knew me well enough to let me have my way.

They went to a friend's house nearby where they could watch. They planned to get me if I didn't get a ride right away.

Within ten minutes I had a ride to Danville in a lovely Buick. There were already three hitchhikers in the car. Two went to Indianapolis; the third, a professor, went to the airport to get a plane from Champaign.

At Danville I hitched a ride to my daughter Hazel's house in Rantoul. I can't describe her displeasure with her mother when she learned my mode of travel. My hitchhiking was embarrassing to my children. I didn't stay long because, by this time, I was anxious to get home. I wondered if Ed would show any concern or signs that he cared about me. I felt better about myself; I thought I could handle whatever lay ahead.

It was a cold confrontation. Ed was more determined than before. Absence had not made his heart grow fonder. He told me to "get out."

My heart sank and I felt my body crumple. I summoned enough courage to answer, "I'm not getting out just like that!" I strained to hold back the tears. "I don't believe in divorce," I told him. "You can get a divorce, but I won't get one. I'll go away and you can have your divorce on grounds of desertion." My words echoed back at me. They were frightening.

In the succeeding days, I determined to follow through on what I said. I didn't know where to go or what I would do. I remembered that God is faithful.

It was many years later that I allowed the Lord to remove the bitterness I held in my heart toward Ed. When it was gone, I was able to say that Ed was a fine man, and I knew that I loved him.

CHAPTER FOURTEEN

Defense Work

"Behold I am with thee and will keep thee
in all places whither thou goest."
                    —Genesis 28:15 (KJV)

If I was to go away for a year, I would need a job. During World
War II, young men had to enlist for military service and when they
left their homes, they also left their jobs. Women took their places.
Women also took jobs in defense plants. In order to work, Mother
and I secured our birth certificates, which we had never had before,
and were then able to get Social Security cards. She planned to find
work near home while I went elsewhere.

I heard that some women in Bloomington were going to Rock
Island, Illinois, to work in the arsenal there. So I went with them.
We got jobs immediately. Six weeks later, three women were needed to go to the Finger Lakes Region in New York State to take charge
of ammunition and supply stockrooms for the Army. I volunteered
and was chosen to go.

We were sent by train to the Seneca Ordnance Depot at Romulus.
It wasn't long before I had learned about my new location. Arsenals
were spread over acres and acres of land in the Finger Lakes Region.
I was shocked by what had been done to make room for the project.
Lovely homes, huge old trees, and undergrowth along the lakes were
removed. Bulldozers had cleared and leveled the land. I wondered
why this lush landscape was chosen when there were expanses of
barren land available. But the transcontinental railway was nearby,
expedience prevailed, and that was the answer. This was wartime.

The buildings—1,000 feet long and 200 feet wide—amazed me.

They held dangerous explosives which kept the nearby residents in constant fear of an accident.

I was in charge of a main stockroom filled with Army tanks, jeeps, ammunition and equipment. I was assigned to a big office and had my own desk. My job was to prepare orders in advance for shipments to be made at a moment's notice.

I found a place to live with a 70-year-old spinster, Corna Everet. She was an independent character like me. She lived in a charming two-story house built by her father for his bride. Corna had lived there all her life and inherited the house when her parents died. Corna had no suitors because she was too "sot" in her ways, she said.

During the war, families were encouraged to raise their own produce, so in the spring, Corna and I planted a vegetable garden. Working the ground was difficult with only a small wheel plow to use. I was strong as an ox and harnessed myself to the front of the plow frame with a rope crossed over my chest. Corna held the handles and pushed with all her meager strength. It took both of us to get the plowshares into the soil.

She would call "gee" or "haw," depending on which way she wanted me to turn, and I turned. We laughed till we cried.

Once when I stopped for breath, I noticed the sunlight glinting on a small object in the soil. I stooped and picked it up. Corna examined it. It was a Civil War uniform button.

"My father's regiment," she said, her eyes filling with tears.

I didn't pursue the subject at the expense of a daughter's painful memories, but quickly became a work horse again.

Later she told me that her father, Doctor Everet, served in the Union Army. On Decoration Day, she always watched the parade as it passed her place on the way to visit the graves of soldiers who died in the War Between the States. Her father's was one of them.

Corna hated war because she lost her father. She resented the ordnance plant workers, too. I was glad she tolerated me.

There were other buttons in the soil and, ordinarily, I would have picked them up because I had a collection, but this was not the time to do it. Once the seeds were in the ground, it was too late.

The year passed and I went home to Bloomington, but Ed had not gotten the divorce.

CHAPTER FIFTEEN

Left Alone

"Let me find grace in the sight of the Lord."
—*Genesis 33:13 (KJV)*

I had spent a year away from home to give Ed grounds for divorcing me, but he hadn't gotten around to doing it. My conclusion was that I would have to go away again.

I heard that International Business Machines (IBM) was hiring people at their electric typewriter plant in Rochester. As soon as I could, I left for New York again.

Even though I didn't know what a typewriter looked like, I was confident that, with my mechanical background, I could manage typewriter assembly.

I was hired at IBM and put on a production line responsible for adjustments. There were 14 people at the table.

A man who sat next to me was irked that I, a woman, ranked above him on the assembly line. He was a good mechanic and could have handled my job. His irritation grew more each minute. Finally, he got up and went to the boss. I knew something was about to happen.

He complained to the boss that I was not doing a good job, perhaps embellishing his story with falsehoods. When I saw the boss coming directly toward me, I was ready to defend myself, and I got my words out ahead of his.

"Wait a minute, before you bawl me out like I know you are planning to do. Look first at the machines we haven't touched, and you'll see where the trouble really is."

There was a woman at another table who also wanted my job, and I knew it. She deliberately put parts on loosely and planned to blame me for it. She was fired there and then, and it didn't bother me a bit. The man stayed where he was and did not oppose me after that. I felt the Lord had watched over me and helped me to keep my job.

I enjoyed the city of Rochester. As a child I had learned from Mrs. Scott's library that there were many things to see in the world, and Rochester held some of them.

On one of my days off, I rose early and took a bus to Lake Ontario. I climbed a power pole to get an uninterrupted view. By now, I wore my work pants everywhere except to church, and I found it much different than when I had to climb a pole for the telephone company in Cooksville in a dress. I didn't care if folks were shocked by seeing me on the power pole, as long as I didn't miss seeing anything.

I went various places on my days off. I visited museums and the University of Rochester. Sometimes I rented a horse and rode to Kodak Park.

Most of all, I enjoyed going to church. It was my soul's fulfillment to be with other believers. The Sunday School class had about 200 members. The church building was also much larger than the one I belonged to in Bloomington.

One time in church, I embarrassed myself as I sat down in my pew. I was so used to wearing pants that I automatically pulled on my dress as I would have on pant knees when I sat down, and my dress came up to my thighs. I hastily put it in place but couldn't concentrate on the service knowing other people had seen me.

I was asked to teach a Bible class of 50 older women in the church. They were supposed to sing hymns, but there was no one to play the piano. The ladies kept insisting that I play, but I knew I couldn't do an adequate job and refused. They thought I was just being modest, so I showed them that they couldn't sing with my playing. They never asked again.

At IBM, I was promoted to a better job. When I realized they were training me for a long-range position, I had to tell them I would not be staying permanently; they should be training someone else. However, for my part, the promotion helped to restore some self-

A fine man.

esteem I had lost through the years.

Winter came bringing snow and curtailed my outside activities. There was always confinement when the factory closed during blizzards. The cold dragged into spring, and I resumed my tours around Rochester.

One day in early fall, I received a long envelope addressed in Ed's handwriting. Inside was a copy of our divorce decree. I looked at our names typed in at the top. I could not help reflecting. Thirty years before we had been lovers; during the years between, incompatible. Both of us at fault. Neither seeing the way to make things right.

Ed included a note:

Oct 11 1944

Grace!—
There isn't anything to say but I want you to know I tried terribly hard before you left — and after you were gone. To try further would be adding insult to injury and would only mean your leaving again. It is no fault of yours and I sincerely hope the future will bring you compensation for the past few years!

Ed.

I went home to Bloomington. I lost track of Ed, but the children kept in touch.

Mother, in spite of her age at 84, was still able to do a day's work. While I was away, she had a fall and broke her leg. She was lame after that. She needed someone, and I was glad to be with her.

I attended church again and was asked to teach a young married couple's Sunday School class named the DKC Loyalty Class, after the Reverend Donald K. Campbell, who had organized it. Through the Lord's help, I was able to share my hard experiences in ways that were profitable to those couples. Sometimes, I added a little of my dad's Kentucky humor to the lesson.

It was an active class as was the church. One night we had 45 foreign students in for a covered-dish supper. Thirty-five were Chinese who were brought to this country in a group of 400 to study airplane mechanics at Chanute Field in Rantoul, Illinois. Seven other countries were represented that night as well. With the world at war, it was a thought-provoking evening.

My mother in her riding habit speaks to an intruder.

I began to work at the Bloomington telephone office making metal plates. I ran the addressograph machine and occasionally did bookkeeping.

I was delighted when I earned enough money to buy a White treadle sewing machine for my mother but was disappointed to find she was unable to use it because of her lame leg. She kept house for the two of us, since she knew housework was not my favorite thing to do. We were together two years.

One morning Mother trimmed the shrubs in the yard and put the cuttings into an old oilcloth. When I came home for lunch, she asked me if I would dig a little ditch around the house to keep the rain water from seeping into the basement. Because I would have had to change my clothes, then change back again, I left it for her to do. After lunch, Mother made the ditch. She leaned down to pick up the cuttings she had put in the oilcloth.

"When I get these picked up, I will be through for the day," she said. But Mother was through right then. She went limp, and I saw her die.

I could have blamed myself, but the effort probably had no bearing on when she died. After her funeral, I found myself alone.

I continued to work for the telephone company, but the job was not fulfilling. Sometimes I drove to Colfax to see Mother Small. The years had mellowed our relationship. To me, she was a balm to a wound we both shared. The time spent together always did me good.

However I tried, I was restless. There was more to life than sitting in a building day after day. I thought of my childhood: I was like a bird on the wing. I felt the need to fly away.

PART II

Over the Mountains

Blithely,
her spirit flies over the rumpled earth.
To fear,
it throws its head,
never permitting a doubt to root—
to thwart—the newfound freedom.

CHAPTER ONE

I Reach the Coast

"I am the Lord thy God . . . which teacheth thee
by the way thou shouldest go."
> —Isaiah 48:17 (KJV)

I directed my way toward the West and spent a week with my daughter, Hazel, in Albuquerque, New Mexico. However, most of June 1947 was spent sight-seeing in that state and the state of Arizona. I saw trading posts, Indian pueblos, a movie site, the Painted Desert from Lookout Inn, and I spent time at the Grand Canyon. There were many special trips as I was able to get rides with tourists. Most of my way was paid for me.

On the 27th, I went back to Hazel's. Of the $64 I started with, I had less than five left. I didn't let her know how low my funds were, but it weighed on my mind. I had doubts about going on. However, I reasoned the money would go no farther if I went back to Illinois than it would if I kept going.

The Lord's words to his disciples came to me: "Go your ways . . . carry neither purse nor scrip." This was the assurance I needed to keep going.

I dressed as though I were going to church; my navy blue hat and gloves coordinated with my light blue dress. Ready, Hazel reluctantly took me to a place on the highway where cars could stop easily. I knew it embarrassed her to leave me with a long line of motley-dressed hikers.

I went to the far end of the row, upended my suitcase, and sat on it. I was expected to wait my turn, but every time I saw a car I wanted to ride in, I stood up and put up my thumb.

I was chosen first. It was a nice looking car, but when I got inside I discovered that there were many extra little gadgets and panels on the dash. It came to my mind that I was in an unmarked patrol car. I figured I was in trouble. It was illegal to hitchhike in New Mexico, and I had no money to pay a fine.

Fortunately, the deputy sheriff was off duty. He had just taken three unruly boys to a reform school. They were products of parental neglect and the concerned deputy was emotional over the matter. He blamed their problems on their mothers who had not stayed home to care for them. He thought all women were alike, and I think he picked me up to vent some of his anger out on me. Even though I wasn't guilty, it was probably good for me to be chided. I was glad he didn't arrest me. He took me to downtown Gallup, and I walked to the west end of town.

Even though I purposed to choose nice cars and, hopefully, interesting people to talk to, I forgot and climbed into an old car, and it was dirty besides. It was loosely packed with soiled clothing. The driver was unshaven, and one hand was missing.

Most of the way was boring, and I slept or blanked it out of my mind. He planned one side trip to Lake Mead, and I was glad to get to see it. However, I was quite concerned for the tires on his car; they were no good according to my experience with tires. Also, the man, anxious to get to a job in Oakland, California, had had no sleep. Except for gas and oil, he never stopped. When we arrived in Oakland, he let me out at a city bus stop.

I paid bus fare to the YWCA and got a room. Since it was Friday, July 4th and businesses were closed, I did some Fourth of July celebrating. I went to Lake Merritt in the heart of the city and mingled with the crowds at Lakeside Park.

Saturday, I got a one-day job with an automobile supply house putting labels on bottles of car polish. I had borrowed money from a lady at the Y and I wanted to pay her back.

On Sunday, I went to church and Monday to the employment office. There I got the "run-around." I was an old woman who had worked only at men's jobs.

Trusting the Lord to help me, I applied for a job at an addressograph office. Through that contact, I got full-time work running addressograph machines for the city water company. They gave me an advance to cover rent and meals.

Next, I got involved in church work in Richmond with 200 students from the University of California at Berkeley. They met in the recreation hall of a housing unit. Their purpose was to start a Sunday School. I was given a class of small, delightful boys, and I also helped with refreshments.

A year passed, and I became anxious to see more of the West. I gave notice to my employer. I forgot that I had signed up to attend a Bible conference at Mount Herman, so I had to get another job in order to pay my registration.

I got on at the Oakland Airport with Airmotive Corporation for a six-week period. After the conference, I used an unusual method to choose where I would go next. I placed a map of Washington State on the table, shut my eyes, and let my index finger drop onto the map. When I opened my eyes, my finger was pointing to Olympia. I took a bus because, in a year's time, I had accumulated more than I could carry.

CHAPTER TWO

What a World ... The West!

"Delight thyself also in the Lord, and He will give thee the desires of thine heart."
—*Psalm 37:4 (KJV)*

I arrived in Olympia on a Saturday and took residence at the Y. On Sunday after breakfast, the lady in charge took me to church, and I just let things happen. There, I met a woman who thought she and I ought to eat Sunday dinner at a restaurant on her bus route. Then, I could ride the bus back to the Y. On my return, I stood at the bus stop. I don't know why anyone would have thought I was hitchhiking without a suitcase, but a fine man came along in a car and asked me if I was. He was on his way south to Portland, Oregon; I decided it would be fun to go. When we arrived, he took me to the Y.

That evening I went to church, worshipped and prayed that God would show me His will for my life.

The next morning I overheard some women talking about a tour of the Mount Hood Loop on the Columbia River. I decided to take the tour before returning to Olympia. I went to the travel bureau and acquired a brochure, but the price was too much for me. Instead of turning back, I went the only way I knew to go.

I took a city bus to the highway going east and put out my thumb. In a few minutes I had a ride. I observed with pleasure the rugged immigrant route along the Columbia River. I could not help admiring the engineering of the road, which contrasted so sharply with the flat roads of Illinois.

From Crown Point I viewed the great Columbia River, the mountains over on the Washington side, the many shades of blue and slate. I tried to imagine how the river had impressed Lewis and Clark.

My thoughts were interrupted by a little puppy wiggling about my ankles. I knew if I paid attention to it, I would meet the owner.

He was a clean cut young man about 23 on his way to a job on the Bonneville Dam project. He invited me to ride with him as far as Multnomah Falls.

He drove an old, dirty panel truck, and the passenger seat had been replaced by a wooden box filled with dishes and pans. He apologized as he showed me where I would have to sit, and I climbed in.

At this moment, I was conscious of what I was wearing. I had a tailored gray suit, black slingback pumps, and a $25 black hat trimmed with roses perched on my newly permed hair. I carried a black corded handbag.

We went to Bridal Veil and Horsetail Falls and followed the rugged trails. I had to tie my shoes on with handkerchiefs. At one point I lost a heel. This was a lot of hiking for a 51-year-old lady dressed for church.

Time passed too quickly, and it was suppertime. I should have been back in Olympia. The young man demonstrated his culinary skills by heating some beans and hash over a camp stove. History came alive and I was suddenly one of the characters in a book . . . out West.

The young man wanted to take me back to Olympia, and we crossed the river to the Washington side at the first opportunity. By that time it was getting dark. An eerie flash of lightening circled the horizon. It fascinated us, and we stopped to watch as more appeared. Soon it was too dark and too far to go on.

He had his bed made up in the panel truck and let me sleep there. He wrapped himself in a blanket and slept on the ground with his puppy. Drifting off, I reflected on covered wagons rolling single file. I also remembered Cooksville, Illinois, and "That Williams Girl" of so long ago.

In the morning, the vast panorama of the Columbia Gorge, golden with sunight, cleansed my soul. I felt so good that I could only believe the Lord had planned the event just for me.

We traveled as far as Yakima, and the young man took me to the

Y. He knew I could make my way from there.

I was tired. I sat in the lobby in a rather loose and informal manner, the heel off my shoe. I felt ill and looked it. I was observed by the woman in charge. She asked if I wanted a job. I said, "No, but if one was offered me, I would take it."

She told me about a housekeeping job with a very fine family that lived in a beautiful section of town. I didn't want housework, and the thought of working in a lovely home with happy people was too overwhelming and foreign to me. I put my foot in my mouth when I said I would take a job if it were offered.

I tried to think of a way out. I had no recommendations, of course, and I thought surely I would not be hired without references. I talked to the woman on the phone. Did I drive a car? Did I like children? My answers were yes, and the woman, Mrs. Peretta Warner, came to see me. I tried to appear ignorant, and though I thought I did a good job, it was to no avail. The woman was desperate. She had tried to get help for a long time and insisted on taking me to see her home on Observation Drive. The house was exquisite, with panoramic views from every window.

She offered me an exceptional salary which included the use of a new Oldsmobile. Because I loved cars, the provision broke down my defenses. I took the job.

But I became ill and had to tell Mrs. Warner. She insisted that I go to bed. In the meantime, she had my shoe repaired and when I was well, she gave me bus fare to Olympia to get my belongings. I had been gone so long that the woman in charge of the Y was at the point of calling the police to report a probable casualty.

I had months of pleasure working at the Warners'. Some of the time I was part of the family and traveled with them. At other times, I was left to do as I pleased. I used the Oldsmobile for errands, grocery shopping and transporting the children. When I was free to go for my own pleasure, I used my thumb. I hiked to Ellensburg, Washington, to see a rodeo, to the Pendleton Roundup in Oregon, and to the "Happy Canyon" pageant put on by the Indians. Once I went to Coeur d'Alene, Idaho, and returned by way of the Grand Coulee Dam.

After a year, I had had enough of housekeeping and decided to go back to California. The time with the Warners was rewarding,

An air view of 107 Observation Drive, Yakima, Washington, 1948-49.

but it was only the beautiful panoramic view from the kitchen window that made dishwashing bearable.

When I left, the Warners took me to Hood River, Oregon, on a family excursion. There they left me at friends of mine who had moved up from Berkeley.

Thinking back, I decided not ever to choose a place again by blindly pointing to a map.

CHAPTER THREE

At Home in the West

''Yea, the sparrow hath found a house. . . .''
—*Psalm 27:5 (KJV)*

My friends in Hood River were from the Sunday School in Berkeley. I intended to say a brief hello, but they insisted I stay and help with, of all things, the housework, so they could finish some carpentry work on their kitchen cabinets. Love for friends goes a long way and I stayed a week.

When I got to Salem, Oregon, the cherry blossoms were billowy white against the blue sky. I fell in love with cherry blossoms when, as a child, I sat reading in the cherry tree in Cooksville. I decided to stay.

I got a job selling magazines and went to Oregon City, Hood River, and The Dalles for three months. There were acres of fruit trees in blossom on the rolling hills in this area. When the tree blossoms were gone, roses greeted me at nearly every door.

That job over, I rented a room in Salem near the business district. I located a church that suited me, and when Monday came, I got a full-time job with Sperry and Hutchinson. I was made manager and held the job for five years.

I bought a house, put in a lawn and built a fence. I added a 15-by 32-foot porch and ceiled the garage to make a room. I had a home.

I gave my job everything I had so, at one point, my job had me. I was fed up with employees who didn't follow rules, and I walked out one Friday night, intending to quit.

It was winter. I started hitchhiking for California. Ahead was deep snow on the Siskiyou Pass. I watched for a car that would be certain

The manager of Sperry and Hutchenson in Salem, Oregon (1952).

to have a heater in it. It also had to have California license plates so I could be sure it would get me over the pass. I turned down every offer until a car came that met the requirements. The driver was a businessman going to Los Angeles.

I could hardly believe it when he told me his name was Luck. It crossed my mind that "things don't just happen, they are planned." God has a will in all things, and I hadn't consulted the Lord about what I was doing. I told Mr. Luck that I had just left a job without informing my boss. When we got over the pass out of the snow, he slowed the car and stopped. To my surprise, he opened the door for me to get out.

"Go back to your job," he said. "If you want to quit, do it decently. You tell your boss."

He was right. Chagrined, I got out, crossed the highway, and began to work my way back to Salem. For me, to change direction was hard and very out of character.

I got home before I was missed and had plenty of time to evaluate my circumstances. I had been wrong to leave the way I did, and God hadn't let me get away with it. After all, I knew He had provided the job for me.

During the years I worked at Sperry & Hutchinson, I earned many vacation periods, and I used them for travel.

Thanksgiving of 1951 I accepted an invitation to visit friends in Santa Cruz, California. When I left, I was at ease in heart, but two drivers told me such sad life stories that I could not help from feeling their pain.

A young Korean veteran in a fine car gave me a ride. He had an arm and a leg missing. Bitterness was lined on his face. He was ready to pour out his thoughts to someone he didn't know.

His words came in torrents, sometimes jerkily, as he relived what happened to him in Korea. He used foul language and expressed his contempt for the U.S. government, the officers who were over him, the past, the present, the future. He was going to leave America and go to Australia.

His mind was so far away that I was sure he drove unthinkingly. He seemed to have forgotten I was there. When he was through talking, he remembered that he needed to put some oil in the car. I saw that it wasn't easy with only one arm, but I was sure he didn't want a woman's help, and I wouldn't tell him that I had had lots of experience with cars.

When we were going again he was quiet. By putting in the oil, he had demonstrated that he was capable. I began to ask about the bright side. He had a wife and children. He owned a good paying business; he had a nice home; and the government had provided him with a specially equipped car. When I asked him what he knew about Australia, it wasn't much and he appeared to lose his enthusiasm about going there. I was glad to get to a junction for another ride.

The second ride was with a salesman. He lived in Sacramento, drove a fine car, and had a wife and children. I spoke briefly about the troubles the veteran had gone through, and the salesman became very quiet. When he finally spoke, he told in sequence a hair-raising story of his life.

He was born in Russia. As a child he had known parental love, but he had witnessed the murdering of his parents and seen everything of value confiscated from his home. A relative had rescued him and taken him to China. Eventually, he was brought to America. I noticed that he was not bitter. He was joyous for America and the goodness of God.

Comparing the two men, they each had great losses. Only one was thankful. Because of their stories, Thanksgiving was special for me because I had much to be thankful for.

Another vacation, I took a scenic cruise on the Princess Marquinna. It was in 1952. She was the smallest and oldest mail boat in a fleet that sailed from Victoria, British Columbia, to Chamiss Bay, Alaska, and the only contact those people had with the outside world. The boat carried all manner of freight. At one point there were three automobiles loaded on to be taken 30 miles because there was no road. A sick man on a stretcher was taken on board to be put off at a mission hospital. Goslings, hens, a dog and sheep raised a cacophony on deck.

The Princess could not dock at Indian settlements built near shallow water. At Clo-oose near Barmanak Point, Vancouver Island, British Columbia, she blew her whistle and Indians came out to meet her in anything that would float. They often overloaded their fragile craft and nearly sank.

We docked at Kilonam's Cannery, saw a floating logging camp, and were able to go ashore at some of the ports. We didn't dare go far because when the Princess blew her whistle, those who didn't board immediately were left behind.

After the cruise, I traveled around British Columbia and Seattle. I walked the full length of the suspension bridge at Vancouver, and the next day went to Peace Park between the United States and British

Columbia. Before I returned to Salem, I determined to save for another boat trip.

That same year I was drawn to make a quick trip to Illinois. There were four states to cross, so I allowed five dollars for each state.

The day I left was beautiful. I quoted the lines from *The Vision of Sir Launfal*, "What is so rare as a day in June? Then, if ever, come perfect days." I thought of the Lord's goodness to me and was thankful for health and opportunity.

One of my rides was with a man on his way to release a crate of homing pigeons. He told me about leg bands, time clocks, and the dangers to which those beautiful birds were exposed. I found that, like my chickens, each pigeon had a personality.

Another ride was with two women driving to Illinois. They had already been driving two days and two nights, taking turns at the wheel. They were tired before they started, having watched beside the bed of a dying relative. At death, the body was shipped ahead, and they were going to the funeral. It was dangerous for them to be driving as tired as they were. I didn't want to take the risk so I told them I wanted to sleep one night. They let me out at Boise, Idaho.

Once I waited for a ride in an electrical storm. A couple rescued me and took me to a hotel where I stayed the night. The next morning my ride was in a car with the radio tuned to Queen Elizabeth's coronation.

That night I was in Cheyenne, Wyoming. I believed the Lord had something special for me to do the next day. I anticipated it, but didn't know what it was.

I rose earlier than usual, packed and, with a spring in my step, took off for the edge of town. Another early hiker offered to carry my suitcase, then he walked beyond so that I could have the first ride.

A young girl in a Pontiac stopped and asked me if I was a hiker. She was driving to Wisconsin from Colorado. She was very tired and wanted company.

We had not gone many miles when I concluded that she was a very poor driver. I never openly criticized a person's driving, but I asked to be let out at the next town. She protested, "I understood you were going to Illinois."

"Yes, I plan to do just that." I was trying to be polite, but she pressed me for my reason. I had to tell her the truth, that her driving was the worst I had ever seen.

The girl confessed that she had never driven on a highway nor for very long at one time. The car belonged to her parents. She was on her way to attend a church school until her boyfriend got home from overseas. She begged me to stay and tell her how to drive.

For her sake, I stayed. I concluded that her parents were praying for her safety, and I was the answer; this was the work the Lord had for me.

For the next few miles, I kept bracing myself to keep from bumping the windshield. My legs were quivering with exhaustion. There was gradual improvement in her driving as I coached her. At Boone, Iowa, we stayed overnight. The next day she let me out at the junction where she turned north. Her driving had improved, and I was sure she would safely reach her destination.

My arrival in Bloomington was a surprise. My daughter, Adrid, had looked after the house. With her permission, I gathered a few belongings that in time had taken on new value. I hoped they were there, because they were the main reason for my trip. I stayed three days and saw a few close friends.

Turning westward, I took in all the sights available. In Mitchell, South Dakota, a couple took me to the Corn Palace; I got to see Mount Rushmore in South Dakota because a man I was riding with let me choose his route to Montana. He had been drinking and when he stopped for more liquor, I left him. A couple with a 15-year-old daughter on their way to Great Falls, Montana, by way of Yellowstone Park took me with them. They stopped at every viewpoint. Heavy floods changed their plans and they went to Coeur d'Alene, Idaho, instead. I went on to visit my daughter Hazel in Spokane, Washington.

From there, I rode with a teacher from Oslo, Norway, driving to Seattle. A few more rides and I was in Oregon at Hood River.

It was evening. The only place to stand was on the edge of the road under the night lights of a tavern. With a prayer, I put up my thumb. I didn't like to hike at night.

A patrol car drove up and the officer asked me if I was actually hiking. I told him "yes." He said he would return soon, and I had better not be standing there when he got back. Leaving, he muttered something that sounded like, "Women!"

I took the first ride. Two young men and a girl in a dirty old car took me to Portland and to a bus stop. The driver was a speed demon and made the telephone poles look like teeth in a fine-toothed comb. When I bought a bus ticket in Portland, thoughts of home were mighty attractive.

CHAPTER FOUR

Alaska

". . . in the time of trouble He shall hide me in His pavillion. . . ."
—*Psalm 27:5 (KJV)*

It would seem reasonable that with a nice home and a good job, I would be content. Well, I was until a widower at church began to pay attention to me. The thought of having a home plus a husband got into my mind and wouldn't leave. He had a teen-age son in high school, and I considered that, in time, the son would go his own way.

Early in my story, I referred to the fact that I didn't know how to choose a mate. I proved it once, and I proved it again. I was not in love—I was in love with love. The man asked me to marry him, and I didn't wait, even to ask the Lord about it, to say "yes." We were soon married.

The father and son moved into my house. The man had an income and began to pay my house payments. I quit my job so I could be at home.

In a short while there were signs of an ulterior motive for this man's wanting me to marry him. I noticed that he had a fear of losing me, and I wondered why. He went "overboard" doing extra things. Then I learned that he was dying of a congenital disease (Friedreich's ataxia, a degenerative disease in which the nerves no longer properly control muscle movement). His son, in time, would die from it, too. I was in line to be a caretaker. Had I known the situation, I would never have married this man, because I do know I am not the kind of person to live an imprisoned life.

Though I was against divorce, in five months from the marriage

91

date, I had instigated one. This is a part of my life I would like to have omitted. Few people knew about it, and that was the way I wanted it to be. I took back the name Small.

I didn't have a job, and I couldn't keep up the payments on my house. While I worked at a few small jobs, I realized I didn't want to live in Salem any longer. I lost my home and sold my furniture.

I had saved for a trip to Alaska in response to an invitation from Ted and Jean Cox in Fairbanks. Jean's mother was a friend of mine in Illinois. I thought I might get a job in Fairbanks and get away from the past.

I sailed from Seattle the 20th of August, 1954, on the *S.S. Baranof.* I was trusting again that God would take care of me.

The shipboard meals were delightful. They included gourmet foods, hors d'oeuvres, soups, fish entrees, roasts, vegetables, salads, cheeses, desserts and drinks. I knew how to enjoy plain food, but it was most pleasant to be served elegantly.

On the twenty-second, we docked at Ketchikan, and on the twenty-third at Petersburg. We had four hours for sightseeing. At 2 p.m. we sailed again, passing many points of interest before night-fall: Cape Vandeport, Tevin Glacier, Cape Fanshaw, Five Finger Island Light, and, by 8 p.m., Midway Island Light and Summer Dumm Glacier.

The next day we came through the Stephan Passage. Juneau was our port and across the bay was the city of Douglas. The two waited as with open arms for the *S.S. Baranof.*

I took a room at the Hotel Juneau and went out to look for work. I got acquainted with as much of the local history as I could and walked short distances on wild, dangerous trails. The buildings in Juneau were crude, especially the living quarters. An old Russian church, probably the oldest in Alaska, was still in use. But I found no job in Juneau.

I bought a ticket at the Alaska Central Airlines and took a flying boat to Skagway. Skagway was on my way to Fairbanks and was once the outfitting point for miners during the gold rush days. It was the gateway to the Yukon and Alaskan interiors. Only a handful of people lived in the long narrow valley. Towering, snow-covered mountains guarded the city.

I got a room at the Golden North Hotel. In the morning I enjoyed a ride on the White Pass and Yukon narrow-gauge railroad over the pass. The train had five cars. I ate dinner while riding through the section of the country where Jack London wrote *The Call of the Wild*. It was the kind of nostalgia I enjoyed.

The following day I rode the Canadian Pacific train to Whitehorse. From there I flew on the Canadian Pacific Airline to Fairbanks. So far, the traveling had been wonderful, even though Jean Cox had warned me that the time I chose to come to Alaska was not a desirable time of year. But, in my condition, I could see no farther than the present.

Jean and Ted Cox's home was comfortable, and they had a lovely garden with many kinds of vegetables and flowers. The petunia blossoms were the largest I had ever seen. I was impressed and figured that I would like to get a job there.

Then, one night there was a heavy frost. The garden wilted; beauty was gone. Jean busied herself bringing out boxes of heavy quilts and winter clothes. The ominous activity inspired me to start packing. I was not prepared in any way for an Alaskan winter. I got ready in a hurry to hike out and head for Illinois. Alaska was no place for me.

Ted said I could probably make it to Tok Junction that day, but Jean didn't want me to hike. She insisted that I should go by bus and wanted to take me to the depot. Against her will, she took me to the edge of town. It was the seventh of September.

As I stood, I noticed a few log houses back in the trees across from me. They were small shelters, nothing more. I was dressed in a heavy coat, but my modish black hat with a jaunty little veil was no protection for my head. A cold, penetrating rain began to fall, augmenting what I already knew: I needed to be traveling instead of standing. I thought surely there were others who were anxious to leave the North Country. I didn't know that most of them had left earlier in the morning. The few cars that went by me were already packed with people and their belongings. There was no room for me. I prayed.

It was nearly noon when a man and his wife offered to take me a few miles. It took several more short rides before I arrived at Tok Junction. The Junction was a small place with a hotel and a gas station. I learned later that most of the landmarks on the map were nothing more than that. I decided, because the sun was shining at the time, to go on to what I thought was a larger place.

A lady waved at me going in the other direction, then turned around and came back. She invited me to spend the night with her, because she was going to leave in the morning for Haines Junction. I could ride along. I praised the Lord for His goodness.

We went to a log house that had been built for travelers. It had been the home of a man who knew what it was like to need shelter. But tragedy had struck that afternoon. A tractor he was driving, while doing some volunteer work for a church, turned over, and he was killed. The lady who picked me up was temporarily in charge.

That night, more travelers showed up than the place could accommodate. The first ones were a couple whose quarrel outside could be heard through the thick walls. The woman said, "I will not stay in such a dump." But she did. Another couple had spent the night before in their car and were grateful for any kind of shelter. To me, the logs burning in the big fireplace were a welcome sight.

In order to make room, my hostess made up beds for us in a room where clothes hung drying. I learned that "The Law of the Yukon" states that everyone must shelter those who, otherwise, would be stranded.

The next day we traveled 164 miles. The seemingly endless miles of frontier, with rivers and lakes looking so much like, went by quickly because of this lady's companionship.

At customs, the Canadian official asked me how I planned to get out of Whitehorse. Not wanting to say, "By hitchhiking," I began with, "Well, I've flown."

Before he could question further, he was interrupted by the arrival of a car pulling a large trailer. There was so much inspection to be done that he waved my driver on. I was saved from having to answer any more questions.

That night we stopped at Silver Creek Lodge near Lake Kluane. The place had served as barracks for road crews when the AlCan Highway was built. Although the lodge had not been maintained, it was warm and had a friendly atmosphere. There were workmen who fixed us a meal.

At bedtime I learned that doors along the Alaskan highway were never locked: "Never should a locked door keep a human being from shelter if his life was in danger." I was fascinated to learn these unwritten laws.

The next morning, the lady and I arrived at Haines Junction where we parted company. She was putting her car on the steamer at Ketchikan; I continued south. We had ridden 518 miles together in two and a half days.

I sat on my suitcase again. "No-see-ems" feasted on my legs and I welcomed the next ride.

I learned volumes from people I rode with. There were whole families from California who went to the northland for the summer and south again for the winter. Others, rather than return when school started, stayed and ordered correspondence courses. When I rode in a truck hauling asbestos, I learned how the substance was mined. When we passed a demolished car by the roadside, I learned how a she-bear with cubs had destroyed it. Talking helped pass the time, and I was curious about everything.

My last ride, on a Saturday, was with a geologist who worked in the territory. He told me about his activities with much enthusiasm, explaining things so that I could understand. He stayed at the Laird River Motel and assured me I could get a room there. To me, the place looked like a residence, and the cabins surrounding it like playhouses. It was by no means a rich man's investment, but certainly a place for shelter. The couple who owned it served a family-style supper,and since it had been one of those days that I had missed lunch, the meal tasted extra good to me.

Supper was over when a carload of hunters drove in and demanded to be served immediately. There was little left to serve. What there was was supposed to be rationed until more food was delivered. The "corner grocery" was over 100 miles away. The next delivery was sometime in the next week. A bucket full of fresh game fish sat on the back porch, but it was illegal to serve game fish. The integrity of these folks caused them to deplete their personal food supply of everything that could be quickly fried. The demanding men ate what was served and never knew how grateful they should have been.

I helped the owner's wife with the dishes, and she told me all about Milepost #496. They were very tired. They were on 24-hour demand for gasoline, repairs, food and lodging. They had no time for themselves. She wanted to have a part in a little mission being started somewhere back in the timber, but there was no way she could. People kept coming.

Nearby, at Laird River, was a hot spring which drew crowds of tourists, and laborers had been coming in from bridge work on the road. One family came with three small children. They had been camping out when the cold rain started falling.

My hostess never mentioned the laundry that had to be done. She had a standard washer, but the clothes had to be hung on the line.

Her husband came in as we finished the dishes and told me how his time was spent. He had been up several times the night before to arrange lodging for travelers and to tend the gas pump.

I was so glad I was just passing through. I left hurriedly the next morning for fear I might cause extra work. A heavy downpour had fallen in the night, and it was raining lightly when I left.

CHAPTER FIVE

Wild Flight

"I sought the Lord, and He heard me,
and delivered me from all my fears."
—Psalm 34:4 (KJV)

I walked around big puddles to reach the road. I put a newspaper under my suitcase as I sat it on end for a seat. Cars came an average of one an hour. It was Sunday and I gave praise and thanksgiving as I sat hatted and dressed as one would be for church.

The silence was appalling. There was not a sound. Then I heard something coming through the brush. I recalled the cab that was battered by the mother bear and stories of bears eating from garbage cans. I admit I was anxious to see what would emerge. Out came a large, shaggy, unkempt dog.

Jean had told me that many dogs lived out around the mileposts. They were too vicious to touch, and I was not sure what would happen. The dog sniffed about me as if checking my credentials. I tried to appear calm, even though I resented him. When he left, I was grateful.

Again the silence was broken. This time guns banged in the distance. The echoes reverberated loudly through the trees. Afterward, stillness pressed in on me again. I waited and waited.

Suddenly, loud, unfamiliar cries of birds broke through the silence. I could tell they were convening the way blackbirds did in Illinois before heading south for the winter. They were not far away. Now and then I got a glimpse of them and could tell they were large birds with very long legs, neither geese nor ducks. All at once, as if by an order, there was a tense silence. Next there were a few extremely loud staccato calls. Orders executed, up, up, up, above the trees, circling and wheeling they flew, each into its place in the familiar wedge formation. It was spectacular, a moment to be shared.

I looked back toward the motel and saw the owners on their porch watching with field glasses. Before I could get back to them, the birds were beyond the trees, heading south. I learned the birds were sandhill cranes destined for the Gulf of Mexico. They had regular stopping places along their migration route.

Back on the road, the silence didn't bother me. The breathtaking departure of the cranes was impressed on my mind. Long bills extended cut the air. Long legs, like rudders, trailed behind. They streamlined their way into a ghostly, gray atmosphere, and left behind them a hush. It was peaceful, as if angel wings had passed me by. They were God's handiwork.

The motel owners warned that, without exception, the weather turned bad the day after the cranes' departure. That would have sent chills up my spine, except I believed that the same Great One who conducted the fowl on their flight would also conduct me as I continued out of Alaska, across Canada and several states to Illinois.

A truck stopped and a tired young driver wanted me to ride with him to keep him company. He had come from Anchorage and still had 600 miles to go. He had not stopped to rest and planned to drive through. He was going for replacement parts for an oil company he worked for.

The rain fell hard and continued in earnest the rest of the day. The truck's windshield wipers were broken and when we met another car, mud splashed on the windshield and had to be cleaned off by hand. It was midnight when we arrived at Blueberry where I planned to spend the night. The young man stopped to eat, but he intended to go on. When he fell asleep at the table, the motel keepers forced him to go to bed. I was glad for his sake and mine, too, because I could ride with him the next day.

The rain was not so bad after breakfast. At a little town where the driver turned off, he made every effort to get me to take a bus. He said that because of the "Law of the Yukon," if anything happened to me and it was learned that he had set me off at the roadside, he would not be able to buy gas or get help from anyone if he needed it. I thanked him, but my answer to him was to drive on and not worry about me. Hitchhikers take chances.

The rain turned to sleet and coated my glasses. I could scarcely see the car that stopped for me. Two workmen gave me a ride to a more sheltered place to stand.

The next man I rode with had a local news story. Wolves were in the area killing caribou. He had just dropped the carcass of a mule, laden with poison, from a plane and hoped to wipe out the pack. It was a front-page feature, the way he told it.

To help me along my way, he suggested that I get a ride at a truck terminal. He took me to one at Dawson Creek in spite of the fact that I told him their company insurance would not allow riders. He learned it when he got there. He was very concerned about me and said he knew the rides I got in that area would go only about seven miles—as far as the next liquor store. He took me through town to a place to stand.

It was so cold that I eagerly accepted a seven-mile ride to get out of the elements. The liquor store was there, and it was not a pleasant place to stand. I walked through the little town and went to a police station where it was safe. I was so wet and cold I had no resistance when a ride was offered to me in an old car with three young Canadian soldiers. One was Indian. They were returning to their base in Calgary and had many miles to go.

There were potential hazards with this ride. The car steered badly, the road was slippery, and the driver was a poor one. Things were so bad that one soldier got out at the first town. I then asked to ride between the driver and the Indian in the front seat. Not only was it warmer, but I didn't like being thrust about from one side of the car to the other in the back seat.

The Indian knew the land and thoughtfully tried to put me at ease by pointing out lakes and rivers. He also showed me his beloved reservation, but the driver kept me in such fear that I didn't see all that he pointed out. I saw the lake waves close up as we drove on the muddy road near the shore. I was apprehensive as the driver wallowed through at breakneck speed. Trouble was bound to come. The Indian became uneasy, too, and asked to get in the back seat. When he got there, he covered his head.

The inevitable happened when the driver attempted to pass a road grader. The shoulder was soft and there was not enough room. The car was on its side. Hoping that my 120 pounds would keep it from sliding into a deep ditch full of muddy water, I grabbed the door handle to hold myself in place. The road grader operator came to assist. He looked for wounded passengers and seemed disgusted because we weren't bloody and I wasn't screaming. He stared at me, a calm, white-haired woman holding onto a door handle. I asked him to please open the door gently so I could crawl out without making the car slip into the ditch. The Indian came next, crawling out from under a pile of fallen uniforms. He could not have been more pale.

A car came along with two men who helped us by standing on the running board while the road grader pulled it out. I left the men to do the job and tried to keep out of the operation. Occasionally, I looked back, remembering the wrecked cars I had brought in for Dad. The men were not having much success.

I knew a woman shouldn't boss, but I discovered that the men had not remembered to shift the car out of gear and were trying to pull it backward. I could keep still no longer. I chose my words cautiously, but I think they would rather have torn the car apart than to have a teacherish, old woman tell them the obvious.

Back on the road, we went our wild, careening way again without an inspection to learn if the vehicle had been damaged. One thing was certain. I was going to get out at the next town. In order to get them to stop, I offered to buy their supper. I knew they barely had enough money to get gasoline.

When the driver learned I was not going the next 500 miles with them, he couldn't understand. But the Indian did. He told me, as he carried my luggage to the hotel, that he hoped he would be allowed to drive.

The next morning was full of activity. I slogged through mud and mire like everyone else. In all my years, I had never seen such mud, even in Illinois. The place was called High Prairie, in the Lesser Slave Lake region, and I thought, "If this is high, I wonder what low would be like?"

My shoes were too muddy to get into anyone's car. I found an old coat that had been thrown aside where a truck had gone in the ditch. I dragged it up to the road, wiped my shoes and then used it to stand on. Teachers and children carrying their shoes wore rubber boots as they walked to school. The wife of a school bus driver stopped to ask if I had seen her husband's bus. An empty gasoline truck came along just then and the driver informed her the bus was in the ditch, but that everyone was all right. I got a ride in the gasoline truck.

There was no end to trouble. On the road we met another company tanker which was loaded. We gave him the right-of-way by pulling to the side. Our truck slid sideways in the mud and gravel and went into the ditch. The other driver came back to help. We could only hope the truck would not go farther into the water. We also anticipated help when the road grader came back, but another truck was stuck on a curve ahead of us. It was a long pipeline truck, and the road grader couldn't pass. Besides that, a car was mired down in the road between us. A priest and two other men were struggling to push it through a particularly muddy spot. The other vehicles were assisted before ours, because they were considered to be in worse predicaments.

When we were back on the road, the driver used a little wooden paddle he had made to scrape the mud off his boots so they would not slip off the pedals on the treacherous roads. By this time, I knew why Jean had tried to discourage me from traveling north in the fall. But, looking back, the local color was worth it all.

From that point, the road got better and we made good time. There was still daylight when we reached the north end of the city of Edmonton, Alberta. The driver let me out at a city bus stop and wished me Godspeed.

Edmonton seemed to suddenly arise in the midst of a sparsely populated frontier. It was an enormous city filled with grandeur. People swarmed to buses as the day's work ended. It was a contrast to the rugged terrain I had come through.

I boarded a city bus and told the driver I would make the connections I wanted from a downtown terminal. The conversation was overheard by two young boys who not only knew the bus I wanted, but also the hotel where I wanted to stay. They were eager to help and when we arrived, they ran to hold the bus for me. To their surprise, I ran along beside them, and we laughed. To them, I probably looked, at 59, like someone ready for the old folks' home, but if they thought that, they soon changed their minds. They rode the bus, too, and when they got off, they said I should get off at the next stop.

I learned there was more chivalry in Edmonton. After registering at the hotel, I went out to eat and got lost. I asked a preacher on his way to prayer meeting which way I should have gone, and he went out of his way to walk me to my hotel. Northland people were very kind, I found.

The next morning the sun shone on the mountains surrounding Jasper and Banff. Ducks and geese feasted on floating sheaves from a drowned-out wheat field. I felt the keeping power of God in my heart and continued southward getting rides.

On the way to Calgary, I rode in a fine car and listened to the driver's distressing story. He had contracted to build a section of a highway, and when it was almost completed, torrential rains undermined the road. It broke through under the weight of a large truck. Equipment used to pull the truck out had further damaged the road. There was not enough time to rebuild, and he felt his creditors would not advance him the money to do it. He had just ordered gravel to temporarily repair the road. We detoured around the project onto country roads which had been churned to mud by the traffic. The man must have picked me up to have a listener, and I sympathized.

We parted at Claresholm. With a good rest that night, I was ready to go on the next day.

My driver's license was all that was needed at the customs office going into Montana. After those muddy miles, the rest of the way was easy. Rides were long between the towns. I arrived in Bloomington, Illinois, on the 21st, two weeks after leaving Jean and Ted in Fairbanks.

I thought of the sandhill cranes. They no doubt had arrived at their destination long before. Theirs was a wild flight to escape the hard winter, and so was mine. It was a time to praise.

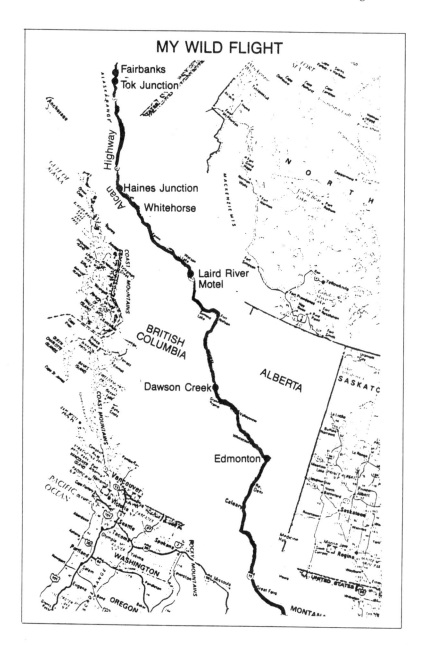

CHAPTER SIX

Getting Settled Again

"I will behave myself wisely . . . I will walk
within my house with a perfect heart."
—Psalm 101:2 (KJV)

With no home to return to, I decided to stay in Bloomington, Illinois, for the winter and be near Adrid who lived at Towanda. To earn money, I worked at everything I could find to do.

At Christmas I worked for the J.C. Penney Company selling yard goods. Later, I was "coffee girl" at Admiral Corporation. On other jobs, I helped put in floor joists and subflooring in a new house, I painted and wallpapered six rooms in an old home; and I washed and ironed clothes. Often, I held two jobs. I did babysitting in the day and odd jobs at night.

In June I hiked to Texas to be with my daughter, Eileen. There I puttied windows and painted frames. When I had done all I could there, I went back to Oregon.

Instead of hitchhiking, I drove a car to Springfield, Oregon, for a used-car dealer. From there I went over to Eugene, three miles away, to see if I could get a job at Robert's Brothers at the Green Stamp Center. I had no problem because of my past experience. I got living quarters with a nurse until I could get a place of my own. Then I bought a small dwelling on south Willamette Street in a very friendly neighborhood.

I still was on the go. I accepted an invitation to a wedding in Nampa, Idaho, I was supposed to ride with friends, but their car broke down the day we were to leave. I was determined to go, so I set out by thumb.

My boss took me to the junction of 99E and 99W in Junction City. Before he could cross the highway to get gas, I had a ride. The ride took me to Portland where I stayed overnight. A man and his wife picked me up the next day. They had seen me hiking at other times and picked me up because they were tired of me making a trip faster than they did. I had heard the same thing from bus drivers. They took me to Eastern Oregon.

Later, another woman passed me, went on and stopped at a light. I thought she was going on, but when the light changed she went around the block to pick me up. "Don't I know you?" she said. "Didn't you manage the Green Stamp store in Salem?" She took me to the other side of town so I could get a ride more easily.

My next ride was with a young man on his way to Fort Sill, Oklahoma, where he was stationed. He told me his problems. He had left his wife in Yakima, Washington, and was hating every mile the further he got away. They had had differences and he had to leave before they could be resolved. He was ready to talk when I got in his car. When I shared some truth with him from the Scriptures, he was encouraged, and though I never heard from him again, I believe he got things straightened out.

Hitchhiking is not safe anymore. When I did it, the people I met were more important to me than any of the places I traveled. Someone was always put into my path who needed encouragement or sympathy or to be shown the value of a Christian life. Lone drivers invariably shared with me when they would, perhaps, never have told their problems to anyone else. I was glad to be on the road to help.

The wedding over, I went back to Eugene to look after my home. I wanted more land, so on April 27, 1956, I bought a small acreage on Echo Hollow Road. I had to pay for the electrical and sewage facilities in advance and then I brought in a small trailer. In May, I built a fence and planted flowers and rose bushes. I had a pasture, sheep, chickens and apple trees. Later the street was paved and curbs and sidewalks poured. In time, I got a larger trailer, a 32-foot Comodore mobile home.

I bought a light blue 1953 Plymouth sedan and named it Little Lycia which means "power to set free." One of the clerks at Roberts Brothers, Gudrun Anderson, was my best friend. "Andy" and I took

A place to call home (1969). I had all the land I wanted.

many fun trips in Little Lycia. We were retired when she died of cancer, and I lost a good friend.

Changing jobs, I went to work in a man's outdoor clothing store, The Workman, on Willamette Street. It was managed by Frank Muhr who found me to be very original in the way I solved problems. He would shake his head as he laughed and say, "That Grace!" The name stuck. When I sent cards on vacations, that is the way I signed my name. There was never any doubt who sent them. I am "that" Grace.

CHAPTER SEVEN

Hiking With Lois

"Thou wilt keep him in perfect peace whose mind is stayed on Thee because he trusteth in Thee."

Isaiah 26:3 (KJV)

When my second cousin, Anna Lois Mills, came west from Somerset, Kentucky, in 1958, I quit a job at Howard Cooper's in Eugene to travel with her for a while. I cleaned their offices, and I wasn't hard to replace. Things were always slow at The Workman this time of year, and so I had the time off anyway.

Lois was born and grew up in the old Mills house in Somerset on Pittman's Creek. As a young child, she knew me as a woman who suddenly appeared and, a few days later, disappeared. Several months or a year would elapse, and then I would appear again.

When Lois came to Oregon, I was 63 years old, 33 years older than she, and since she wanted to learn to hike, I thought I should teach her how. First we took short trips in Oregon to Salem, Portland, Pendleton and other spots. Then we took a long trip across the country to Kentucky and Illinois.

Once, while going east through Texas, we got in a truck with a farmer. Lois sat in the middle, and I was next to the window. I always tried to make conversation with my drivers, and I gestured toward the pampas grass standing tall and beautiful against the blue sky. I wanted to know the name of the plants.

"What's that?" I asked.

The farmer solemnly answered, "Telephone poles."

Lois and I burst into laughter. Every time after that when we saw bunches of pampas grass, we knew that they were telephone poles.

When we hiked together, we went prepared to eat. We took along my usual suitcase and a smaller one which I called my commissary. It contained coffee, cream and sugar. Lois had a small electrical element with a cord that enabled us to heat water. We plugged it into an outlet, put the element in a cup of water and hooked it to the rim of the cup. In no time, the water was hot enough for coffee. When we were near a grocery store, we stocked up on crackers, cheese, peanut butter, and foods that we could eat on the road. With our own commissary, we didn't have to go out of our motel after dark to eat.

On December 29, 1958, we left for Puerto Rico to visit my daughter Hazel. Going east, we planned to visit every friend and relative we knew along the way.

It was cold when we started and drivers picked us up readily. We met my oldest daughter Eileen in Sacramento and stayed with her the first night. The Allens, friends from Bloomington, lived in Anaheim. They kept us for two days and took us to Disneyland.

Day after day, we traveled successfully, getting rides through Arizona and Texas. I had friends in Shreveport, Louisiana, Dr. and Mrs. H.F. Pledger, whom we stopped to see. Our route then took us through Mobile where we again made a brief stop. H.O. and Bessie Wolfe welcomed us. They were also old friends from Bloomington. From there, we went to Marianna, Florida, for the night. Two more nights, one at Avon Park, the next in Miami, and we were ready for our flight.

Sunday, January 10, we flew into the San Juan airport. We spent two hours with Hazel's family at the military base, then she took us to points of interest. After that, Lois and I toured the island by ourselves and felt we were having more fun than any other two people could ever have had.

We were there only one day. That evening we were back at the airport. The plane and crew were the same ones we had flown with in the morning. We were soon sleeping in Miami.

Monday morning, we began our return to Oregon by way of Kentucky and Illinois. We got rides going to Moss Bluff, Florida, where a friend, Marion Brinson, lived. We stayed with her until the sixteenth, visiting and catching up on our writing. We were at Madison Florida, by nightfall on the seventeenth.

January 18 was special because it was Lois's birthday. We arrived in Atlanta in a luxurious car with a wealthy but discontented driver. He told us that he had seen and done everything he wanted and had more money than he knew what to do with. My heart went out to him when he said he didn't want to live any longer.

Learning it was Lois's birthday, he treated us to a special birthday dinner in a lovely dining room. I thanked the Lord aloud for the food and prayed in my heart for the man. I have often wondered what happened to him, and I hope that our lives were a witness—conveying to him that there was more to life than he believed. He paid for a very nice room for us at the Waldorf Motel, and we never saw him again.

We had a very special visit with Florence Senifer, who was the grandmother of Lois's former husband. She was a longtime Christian and one of the sweetest ladies anyone could know. She lived at Harriman, Tennessee. From there we got rides to Pilot, Kentucky, and then bought Greyhound tickets to Somerset. We stayed three days, pulling the past and present together and having a good time.

Next we went to my daughter Adrid's in Bloomington, Illinois. The area was new to Lois, and she enjoyed going along with Adrid and me as we visited friends and several of our relatives. We saw Mrs. A.B. Means, my dear friend in Bloomington. At Colfax, we saw Bill Harness, my Aunt Meg's son. He married Lois's sister and had a little daughter, Anna Jean. So Lois saw a niece she hadn't seen before. At Anchor we saw Henry and Ova Harms whose home had been my refuge during "cabin fever days" many years before when my children were small.

We went to Selma, Illinois, to visit my parents' graves at the Pleasant Hill Cemetery, and also visited the old site of a Kickapoo Indian camp.

Hitchhiking was even yet illegal in Illinois, so we rode the bus from Bloomington to St. Louis. My friend Dorothy Bagnall put us up. I often stopped at her house while hitchhiking and always received an enthusiastic welcome.

The next day we hiked to Little Rock, Arkansas, and stayed at a motel. I sent a postcard to Addie Macon, my neighbor, who was taking care of my mail in Eugene. "The Good Lord surely was with us today, for that snowstorm caught us about the middle of Missouri,"

I wrote. "We got rides, and we arrived here at the Marion Hotel neither wet nor cold. As ever, 'That' Grace." The storm had been mentioned on the national news, so I knew Addie would be glad to hear that we were all right.

The next night we stayed at Garland, Texas, and I sent Addie another card: "Sunshine and warm weather with grass beginning to turn green—some change!"

A cousin, Ruth Williams Kaminski, was waiting for us at El Paso. Carol and Chester Pinder, second cousins, also lived there with their two children. We stayed the night with them.

We had to work our way through a bad windstorm to reach the home of Cousin Jack Mills in Elfrida, Arizona. He and his wife Vera owned a museum with a guest apartment above it. We stayed there.

The museum was full of Indian artifacts they had unearthed at nearby archaeological digs. They took us out and showed us where they had been working. Jack turned up a piece of soil. The ground was cold and produced a strange black blob. Lois picked it up to examine it. She asked Jack what it was. He quickly knocked it out of her hand. He told her that she was holding a scorpion. It was so cold that it hadn't started to wiggle, but it would soon have warmed up from Lois's body heat.

Jack and Vera took us across the border into Mexico. I had never been to Mexico and enjoyed it tremendously.

When we left Jack and Vera's, we hiked to Youngstown, Arizona, where more cousins, Dr. Henry Rich and Tennie Mills, lived. We went to church with them on Sunday.

Several days later we reached my daughter Eileen's house at Rancho Cordova, California. We stayed from February 16 to 20, leaving very early in the morning by way of Mt. Shasta. We had several good rides and got to Eugene by 8:15 p.m. It was a great trip, and we were thankful to arrive safely home.

Lois and I hitchhiked to Yellowstone Park in August of 1959. We saw beautiful country at St. Anthony's Park in Idaho, and we rode with some delightful Jewish folks into Yellowstone. We saw hot springs and volcanoes and took pictures of black bears through the car windows. After seeing Old Faithful, Lois and I both felt the Lord would have us suddenly end our visit to Yellowstone. We wondered why.

Three cousins at the museum in Elfrida, Arizona. From left: Jack P. Mills, Lois Mills, and myself. (February, 1959)

It was a long way to the west exit, and we got a ride with a woman who was a guest at the park. She had a cabin and was going to the store for supplies.

We continued our sightseeing at the Grand Tetons, and we were at Jackson Hole by August 17. That was the date, shortly before midnight, when the Madison River Canyon earthquake shook Yellowstone National Park. It measured 7.1 on the Richter scale, and eight states felt the first jolt. The cabin of the woman who drove us to the exit was in the canyon. It was covered by 400 feet of rock. We assumed the woman was killed. Twenty-eight people died, and 19 of the bodies were never recovered. We had originally planned to stay at Yellowstone, and we knew, for some reason, the Lord protected us by getting us to leave.

We were back in Oregon before the end of August. There were many times when our minds filled with solemn thoughts about the earthquake and our escape.

CHAPTER EIGHT

Escaping the Blues

"To everything there is a season. . . ."
—*Ecclesiastes 3:1 (KJV)*

Midwinter in Oregon always affected me adversely. By January or February, I was ready to get out of the confines of my trailer. There were no flowers to tend in the yard, and going to church, helping in mission work, making quilts, visiting the Eugene Library, and reading books didn't help. I had to get out on the highway and go somewhere. In the middle of February 1960, Lois and I set out for Illinois.

The rides through the Cascades to Bend and south to Tulelake, California, provided new scenery. A good night's rest at a motel got us ready for the road to Reno, Nevada. It was cold, but that was good because it caused drivers to stop and pick us up more often. Arriving in Reno at 3:30 p.m., we decided it was too early to stop so we hitchhiked on to Fallon, Nevada, and spent the night there.

Highway 95 South was readily accessible, and we left early in the morning for Las Vegas. There were few cars and our progress was slow. By the time we got to Las Vegas, we were tired. We got a room at the McDonald Hotel, locked ourselves in and went to bed. In the morning, we prepared for the day, packed our suitcases and started to leave. The door wouldn't open. We locked it and unlocked it. First I would try, and then Lois. In exasperation, we took the hinge pins out of the hinges. Together we lifted the door out.

We explained at the desk how we couldn't get out until we removed the door. As we left, I said, "The door to Room 203 is lying on the bed." Thinking how foolish it sounded, we left hurriedly.

Traffic was light, but we eventually got to Flagstaff, Arizona. There we found snow. In the morning there was more snow, so we took a bus south to Phoenix. There was snow in Phoenix, too, but at least the sun was shining.

It was impractical to go on hitchhiking when traffic was slowed down by the weather, so we decided to stop again and stay overnight. But every room was filled. We took a bus to Mesa to try there, but there were no vacancies. We went on by Greyhound to Globe, Arizona, and finally found a room at the Apache Land Lodge.

On the morning of February 20, the weather looked good, so we set out again. Rides took us to Fort Hancock, Texas, by nightfall.

The next day we had to be very choosy about our rides. My friends, the Scotts, were in Abilene, and they had been told we were coming. We were able to schedule our traveling and reached our destination. We stayed overnight with them, and because Eileen's husband was stationed in Austin, we planned a visit with her. We arrived on the twenty-second, and left on Leap Year Day, February 29.

We made our way to Little Rock, Arkansas, and because there was snow and ice, took a bus to St. Louis. It was too late to call Dorothy Bagnall, so Lois and I adjusted ourselves in seats at the bus terminal and tried to sleep. At least we were warm and dry.

In the morning, we went on by bus to Bloomington and to Adrid's house. We stayed three days.

Heading home, we took the bus back to St. Louis. From there we hitchhiked to Joplin, and the rides came easily. We hoped to get back into the South where the weather would be warmer.

It was still cold. When rain fell and there was mud, we quit hiking and took a bus to Dallas. There we spent another uncomfortable night in the depot, and when we could make connections, we went on to Forth Worth. We hiked from there to El Paso, and the next day headed for the Carlsbad Caverns in New Mexico.

Inside the caves, we went down as if we were going to the bottom of the earth. There we saw a dining room beautifully lighted, chambers and chambers of splendidly formed stalagmites and stalactites. We had a spectacular tour. The guide turned out the lights at one point so we could experience total darkness. I felt the Lord had blessed us in allowing us to see this awesome part of His creation, even though I had seen it years before.

On the way home, we again stayed with the Allens in Anaheim, California, who were glad to see us and get fresh news from Bloomington. The next day we took a bus to San Fernando, and from there bought tickets to Eugene.

We arrived in plenty of time to spend the rest of the day thinking over how we had escaped the last part of winter in Eugene. I was conditioned for spring and flowers. It was March.

CHAPTER NINE

Camp Helfrich, 1962

"I watch and am as a sparrow alone upon the housetop."
                                      —Psalm 102:6 (KJV)

This event in my life was one of the greatest adventures I ever
experienced.

Clerking at The Workman put me in touch with many outdoor
people. One was Prince Helfrich, who was a well-known conserva-
tionist, geologist, naturalist and boy's camp leader. He was also a
river guide on the Rogue and McKenzie Rivers in Oregon and he
pioneered riverboating on many of the western rivers of the United
States.

In the summer of 1962, he had a fishing camp on the Rogue River
in Oregon. He advertised for someone to keep the camp for him during the months of September and October and got no response.

Prince knew me as the Hitchhiking Grandmother, a title given
me in 1960 by Pepper Berkeley in Eugene, a *Register-Guard* reporter,
when she did an article on me. Prince considered what I did daring.

He came into the store, and the idea struck him to ask me to keep
his camp. He looked straight at me, "Grace, I need someone to stay
at my Rogue River camp this fall."

Amused, I looked straight back. "Who are you looking for?"

"Would the job interest you?" he asked.

I had to think. I had never been camping. One thing special came
to mind and that was the fact that Zane Grey's cabin was on the
Rogue River, and I had always wanted to see it. He did a lot of his
story writing there, and I had read his books. Wherever I could on

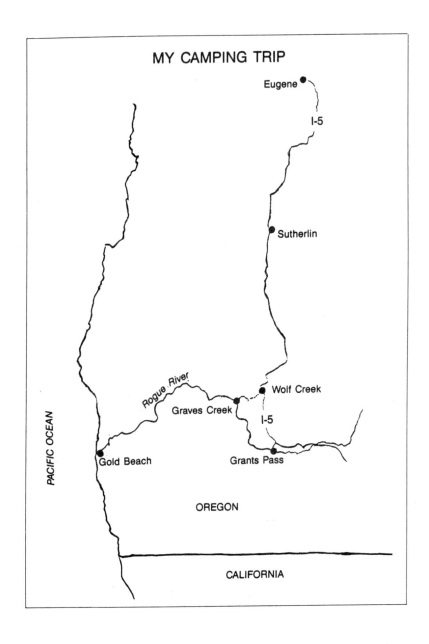

my journeys, I followed his trail. I had thought this famous cabin inaccessible to me.

Prince kept adding things to try to interest me. "You wouldn't have to cook. My sons help do that. You would change the bedding and keep the deer away."

"How close can I get to Zane Grey's cabin?" I asked.

He smiled. "I can get you to the landing at Winkle Bar."

That was all I needed to know, and I took the job.

On Labor Day, Prince arrived at my trailer in Eugene in a red 1959 Chevrolet station wagon. Two boats were stacked on a trailer behind.

For the first time, I wore jeans. I wore a red plaid blouse, heavy, ankle-high leather shoes, and a broad-brimmed straw hat. I felt properly dressed. He loaded my luggage and we took off. I was thinking of Zane Grey's cabin; he was thinking of his camp.

In the midst of boxes packed in the back lay a big brown border collie. "The dog's name is Delmo," Prince explained. "She can help keep the animals away."

I learned later that the dog had been cuffed by a bear, and the blow addled her brain. As a watch dog, she was worthless. If she saw a deer, she might chase it, she might ignore it, or she might run and hide. Prince had purposely brought her to "keep an old lady company."

We stopped at a Sutherlin Station to pick up Prince's helper, Bill Palmer, 16, the son of a Portland lawyer. Prince asked Bill to drive because he had hurt his hand with an ax and wanted to save it for the river. I had not thought about going down the river.

We left the main highway at Wolf Creek on a road through the Siskiyou National Forest. I was fascinated with the huge, old growth timber, but the deep ravines along the narrow road with no guardrails were frightening. Bill worked hard to make every turn, always regarding the trailer behind.

Below, at the mouth of Grave Creek, the men tied the boats and distributed the gear between them. My eyes were on the rapids. What was ahead for me was to be more frightening than the road behind had been. The river drops 1,000 feet between Grants Pass and Gold Beach, a distance of 120 miles. My stubborn pride kept me from backing out.

Delmo went in Bill's boat, and I got into Prince's. I sat gingerly as I held onto my hat. Untied, the boats were snatched from the creek's mouth. I wondered how fast we were going as we passed huge boulders, went over rapids, and between narrow canyon walls.

We portaged at Rainie Falls. Delmo and I walked around the falls while the men let the boats down the fish ladders with hand lines.

It was, however, exhilarating to ride the river, and Prince pointed out things of interest. There were old, weathering, abandoned prospectors' cabins. He knew the ferns and foliage by name. He named the landmarks as we came to them: Tyee, Wildcat, Russian, Slim Pickins, Plowshares, Wash Board, Black Bar Rapids, and Horseshoe Bend. It was at Horseshoe Bend that a wind current caught my hat and I saw the water carry it swiftly away.

Vacationers from Portland, Dr. and Mrs. Allen M. Boyden, with their young son, Allen, were fishing at the mouth of Meadow Creek just above Prince's camp. They owned a cabin up the river a mile. We rowed to them and I was introduced.

Some days before, Dr. Boyden had expressed disbelief when Prince told him he was bringing a woman to watch his camp. He remembered what Prince had said about me: "Oh, wait till you see her! Wait till you see her!" he quoted.

Our boats were soon at the landing. The men set up the cook tent and a tent for me at the far end of the structure.

Prince's sons, Dave, Dick and Dean, had come the day before and set up four tents for guides and guests on a higher level of the meadow, near the foot of a canyon wall.

There was a ground grill and another large fireplace in the center of the camp. Our first meal was hot corned beef hash, carrot sticks, and bannock, an unleavened flatbread or biscuit baked on a griddle. Dessert was sliced bananas mixed with fresh peaches.

That evening we were early to bed and from my cot, I listened as a small plane flew over. Prince explained the next day that it was Deak Miller returning down river to his Paradise Lodge before it got too dark.

The Boydens were going home and brought us peaches and fresh vegetables they didn't want to take back. Margery Boyden told me I would meet a lot of boaters and hikers during the next weeks. Sometimes Prince brought his wife Marjorie. (The wives' names were

Zane Grey's cabin.

the same, only spelled differently.) I knew I would not be lonesome.

The great moment for me to see Zane Grey's cabin came when Prince went to get guests. I rode the rapids again, willing to take the risk. Delmo went, too.

Arriving at Winkle Bar, we stepped out onto the landing. I could hardly believe I was there.

Grey's cabin, a short way across the meadow, was surrounded

by a grove of oaks. It was a long, one-story building, old and weathered. The entrance faced the river. The roof sagged and extended to cover a porch at the front. I walked around. I recalled his stories, and what an avid fisherman he was. He fished the world's best spots, and he had fished the Rogue. The highlight of my trip was over, except for the fall beauty everywhere as we walked the four miles back to camp.

Prince came and went with guests. I was always glad when he brought Marjorie and we could visit. When I was alone, I explored. Once I picked apples at a deserted old house and took them back to camp. In October, the Boydens came again for a few days to close their cabin for the winter.

Prince, Dick and Dave arrived with guests from New York. Prince grilled T-bone steaks and Dick made biscuits. Dave and I made a vegetable salad. When the meal was ready, it rained so hard the men had to eat in their tents. The arrangement was an embarrassment to Prince.

About dark, the rain let up and Prince built a bonfire. Camp chairs were brought and the men exchanged stories far into the night. A transistor radio brought news.

I fell asleep listening to the dripping sounds of water falling off the cook tent. In the wee hours of the morning, something woke me. I peered out. The Helfrichs were going toward the river, carrying lanterns. The river was flooding, and they had to bring the boats to higher ground.

The next morning the canyon was dark. Prince built a fire at the end of the cook tent to add some brightness. Now and then, raindrops sputtered in the flames, and the gray smoke took its time to rise in the heavy air. The breakfast of bacon, eggs and pancakes was not as important to Prince as was the riled, swollen river that made fishing impossible. He had high-paying guests from the East Coast and nothing to offer.

He told the men, "The fish won't bite in this muddy water."

A guest asked if the condition of the river was unusual.

"It is for this time of year . . . much too early," Prince admitted.

The guest was thinking it was a long way to come to fish and have it spoiled by bad weather. "Is our fishing over?"

Prince assured him that they would go into Grants Pass and wait until the river went down.

About then, the rain came in torrents. The men moved swiftly to get onto the river before it got higher. Prince said for me to move to one of the tents above.

I watched six men in bright orange and yellow jackets as they got into the boats. The guides untied and surrendered their crafts to the brown swirling water. An uprooted tree followed them. I was being left alone, but nothing in the world could have made me get into one of those boats. As the men passed a bend down the river, I realized that I was more alone than I had ever been before. No one would be hiking; no one would come by in a boat; I would see no one until the water went down.

I moved to one of the guest tents and did what I could to pass the time. I wrote letters, took pictures, even though the light was poor, and caught rain water to drink.

As the days passed, my food supply got slimmer.

October 12, Columbus Day, shortly after noon, an unusual calm settled over the canyon. The air was as hushed as an actor offstage waiting for his cue. All at once, a heavy gust of wind attacked the top of the trees and died. Then the wind attacked again. It increased, warlike and fierce. The sound of breaking limbs and falling timber echoed back and forth. The force picked up waves from the river and dashed them against the canyon walls. Spindrift blew upstream, blurring the view. It was like a nightmare; something not to be believed; but it was real.

The supports holding the cook tent leaned in the wet sand. The tent flaps whipped wildly. It was dark as dusk, but there was no safe place for a lantern. I grabbed some crackers and ran to my tent for shelter. Behind me, the cook tent fell in a heap.

Delmo, wet, smelly, and with sandy paws, leaped into the tent beside me where she was not allowed. Her bed was outside the door.

I went to bed. I tolerated the dog. Warm and damp, her body gave off odor as she peacefully slept. Despite the booming and crackling of falling trees, I also slept.

Sunlight greeted me. Deer tracks set deep in the sand trailed through the camp. I put the cook tent back in place and built a squaw fire to make oatmeal, toast and coffee.

My loneliness was a problem. There was no one to talk to. It helped to sing, but when I did, Delmo showed disdain. The Rogue responded with roaring while Meadow Creek, almost a river itself, joined in.

Amid the confusion, I detected the sound of a plane. Soon I could see the gleaming red and white colors. It was Deak. He flew over once, then twice. The second time he dropped a canister with a note.

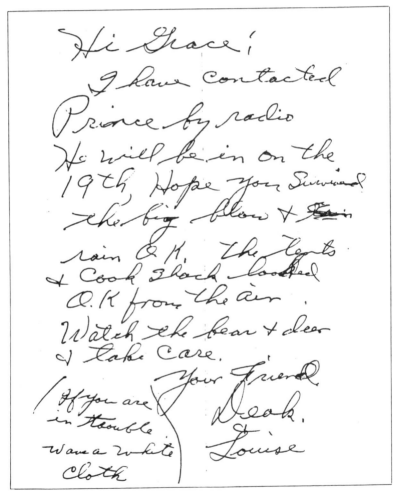

The note dropped from the airplane at the Rogue River, October 13, 1962.

He passed over one more time, but I wouldn't wave a cloth just because I was lonesome.

There were six more days to wait. The previous four had been hard for me. I consoled myself with the thought that at least people were thinking of me. I would have to make do for meals with the little I had.

It can be a frightening thing to be alone and think you hear someone call your name. I heard, "Grace!" And again, louder, "Grace!" It came from the direction of Meadow Creek. I hastened over through the wet, yellow meadow grass. As I looked ahead I saw two forms on the other side of the swollen creek, Allen and Margery Boyden. They shouted, "Are you all right?"

I couldn't help it. Tears loomed in my eyes. Across the noisy waters, I shouted uncontrollably, "I thought I was alone! I am so glad to see you!"

Dr. Boyden explained that we had been through the tail end of a Pacific hurricane. They had heard on their radio that it was coming as they were packing, but didn't have time to get out. To get to me, they had made their way through more than a mile of fallen trees.

"How would you like some fresh deer meat?" Dr. Boyden raised his arm and threw a white package 20 feet across the flooded Meadow Creek. He continued throwing canned foods and some butter, which I needed for biscuits. I had prayed a lot, and my prayers were answered.

It was some time before we got out of our forest prisons, but with the Boydens nearby, those six days were easier for me. It took many crews with chain saws to clear the way, and Prince came back as he promised.

PART III

Over the Sea

Pictorial scenes of distant lands, the love for history, and a young girl's dreams to travel, locked away, emerge and become reality as the lock is broken.

CHAPTER ONE

Never to Europe, 1964

"But the people who do know their God shall do exploits."
—Daniel 11:32 (KJV)

I was content. Selling men's clothing at The Workman, along with my meager social security check, provided enough money for me to do the things I wanted to do. My apple trees and garden enabled me to can my food. I had need of nothing. If I was ever settled in my life it was at this time.

But, one day the young brother of the store owner, Jim Petersen, came in and flashed a passport in front of me. "I'm going to Europe," he announced. With exuberance he explained about all of the preparations he was making to go.

What is so great about going to Europe, I thought. "Mercy me! All I have to do is pack a little suitcase, get out on the road and put up my thumb. I can go anywhere I want here on 20 dollars," I told him. I wanted no part of what he was about to do. But want it or not, I was exposed to his European travel fever.

I was further exposed while I read the scriptures one day. The apostle Paul said: "Whensoever I take my journey into Spain." Spain! It hit me that my daughter Hazel and my son-in-law were stationed in Zaragoza. She had described in a letter some ancient structures still standing that were there during the time of the early Christians. All at once, Spain didn't seem so far away.

A final onslaught came when young friends in Germany sent a newsclipping showing an 80-year-old English woman taking her tenth hitchhiking trip to Italy. "Now you have no excuse, Grace,

. . . please come to see us!" With this invitation, I succumbed.

I had no savings to draw from to take the trip, but I did have a small life insurance policy. Should I use it, or not? I had finally learned that when I wanted to go somewhere, to first ask the Lord. Sometimes His answer was no, sometimes yes, sometimes wait and sometimes go immediately. I was kneeling in a praying position with my Bible open to Daniel 11:32 when these words stood out: *". . . but the people that do know their God shall be strong and do exploits."* I knew God, I reasoned, I was strong, and I *"would do exploits."* This was a positive answer to me. I was going to go to Europe.

I worked through January and a few days in February of 1964 saving money for my venture. Then, The Workman closed, and I was out of a job. It was not a catastrophe; it was freedom to me. I was 68 years old and past retirement age. Looking at my life insurance, there was enough money if I cashed it in for a flight to Europe and back. It seemed the right thing to do.

I was ready a month early and couldn't wait to get started. I acted just as excited as my boss's brother. I left March 5th after 15 church friends gave me a bon voyage dinner party. A Eugene *Register-Guard* reporter came to take my picture and do a feature article about me as *The Hitchhiking Great Grandmother*. By this time in life, I had great-grandchildren.

The words from Acts 8:26 *"Arise and go South"* assured me of my direction to start. I was invited to visit on the way with Louise and Win Baker, friends from Illinois living in Sacramento, California. I stayed there a few days, bought maps, and chartered my route. I had friends and relatives all across the continent I wanted to see.

I asked a motorcycle officer about the flow of traffic at a certain place and my chances to get a ride. He pushed his sunglasses to the top of his head and grinned as he assured me, "Lady, I think you will make it all right." He had viewed my black velvet hat with the veil across the front that made me look like I was going to church. "Stay on the ramps, and when you cross town, take a city bus. You'll get along OK."

I prayed and read the Bible at the begining of every day. I was assured by verses such as Luke 12:24, *"Consider the ravens, for they neither sow nor reap. . . . How much more are ye better than the fowls?"*

Grace Small: 'I'm Allergic to Walking'

From the Eugene Register-Guard, *March 5, 1964.*

On the ninth day of my journey, I turned to my "Guide Book" for instructions: Psalm 26:7, *"That I may publish with the voice of thanksgiving, and tell of all thy wonderous works."* From those words, I knew there was something special for me to do that day.

I waited beside the road with my thumb out, and no one came by. After some time, I wrote in my diary, "No traffic. No coffee. Can pray." Finally, a ride came. It was not a long ride, and I got out at the next junction. The next car that stopped was a man and his wife on their way to Tucson, Arizona. It was a pleasant ride under blue sky, interrupted now and then by the stately saguaro, prickly pear, and cholla cacti. At Tucson they got a motel and the wife asked me to stay with her while her husband went on business. We went out for a late breakfast. She was burdened about her family.

I was able to share *"the wondrous works of the Lord"* in my life. Back in the car, we had privacy to pray. It was 11 o'clock when she drove me to the highway to catch a ride. I received a letter from her the following Christmas in which she quoted James 5:16, *"The effectual, fervent prayer of a righteous man availeth much."* Prayers were answered. The *"wonderous works of the Lord"* were published and I had a *"voice of thanksgiving"* because we met that day.

My thumb was out again when a large car pulling a travel trailer came along. The driver was going to El Paso. I questioned whether I should take the ride because it would mean slow traveling. Also, I had the impression that the driver, a middle-aged man was in the throes of a dilemma. I was about to say "No, thank you," but I hastily observed as much as I could before making up my mind. He seemed educated and had a public address system in the car. Any longer deciding would have been awkward, so I got in.

"You show slides and movies of your experiences," I offered. He didn't answer. "In your trailer you have a study desk and a typewriter for correspondence. You have a projector, screen and film." He listened with no response. My words were bringing him back to the reality from which he had been slipping. Finally, he spoke.

He told me that he was a minister. He and his wife had been missionaries in the Philippines during World War II. They had experienced much suffering. He had spent three years in a prison camp. Now, he was making public appearances and showing slides. His wife was a successful writer for an internationally known Bible publishing company, and they were seldom together. He was unhappy and was considering a divorce. As we talked, he realized that that was not the way for him to handle his problem.

He let me out in El Paso, where I had friends, I never saw him again. But, I knew that our meeting brought another time to "publish with the voice of thanksgiving . . . the wonderous works of the Lord."

In Austin, Texas, March 15, I went to church with Eileen. On Monday, we shopped and she bought me a new dress. The visit gave me time to get reacquainted with my grandchildren. Later in the week, I rode to Waco with Eileen and some other officer's wives going to a bowling tournament. I went on from there toward Illinois.

On the way, a patrol officer picked me up and gave me a free 25-mile ride to a small bus station. "Buy a ticket to Bloomington, Springfield, anywhere! Just get off of my route," he ordered.

As soon as he was gone, I inquired about a bus and learned that there would be none until morning. I bought a cup of coffee and a roll while making up my mind whether to wait or go on. My decision was to go on. I walked to the highway and put up my thumb. A couple in their fifties on their honeymoon picked me up. They took me to Illiopolis, Illinois, where my friends Jerry and Mary Butler lived. They came and took me to their home. My daughter Adrid and other friends lived north of there around Bloomington, and I was anxious to see them.

Adrid and I went to church on Palm Sunday and Easter, and the week with her gave me time to visit.

One of my friends in Bloomington gave me her sister's address in New York City. She notified her sister that I was coming. It was a place I could stay until plane time.

As I left Illinois, I got caught in a miserable snowstorm and the ride that rescued me was a burial-vault salesman. He took me to the address of a friend of mine. But, she was not home. Disgusted with me, he took me to the YWCA and sternly told me to call my son in Detroit and tell him what I was doing. Because he no doubt thought of me as "old," he must have thought my son would discourage me from going to Europe. I did try to call him but was unable to reach him.

My scripture reading that night was Psalm 136, which repeats over and over, *"His mercy endureth forever."* That thought was well drilled into me by the time I finished reading it 26 times. His mercy had gotten me out of the snow, and I knew it.

The next morning I rode with a doctor who considered that I must be in very good health for my years. My second ride was with a young man hauling a motorcyle in a pickup. It was snowing hard, and he wanted me to be his co-pilot to New York. I agreed to help, but after some miles, I discovered that he was very sleepy; it was life-threatening for him to be on the road. His name was Erick, and to ride with him was so frightening that I will never forget him. It was dark when he stopped at a motel restaurant for coffee. I warned him that he should not go on without sleep, but he went and I stayed in spite of his plea for me to go on.

There was no vacancy at the motel, and I had to stay up all night in the restaurant. The woman who was night manager and her husband owned the business. She was very glad to have me stay, because "maudlin, shady customers frequented the place."

During the night, there was one fine young man who came in. He kindly secured a map of New York City for me, and I spent much time planning how to find the places I wanted to see. I had a week to spare, and I knew I could take several excursions including Columbia University, a place I had always wanted to see.

In the morning, the manager's husband arrived and advised me to take the commuter train into the city, then take a bus and give the driver the address of my friend's sister. He took me to the train, and I did as he said. To my surprise, my bus went to the Columbia University campus and stopped in front of Concord Hall.

"This is 468 Riverside Drive," said the driver. I couldn't believe it was the correct address. The bus driver didn't either. But I was to stay on the campus.

I was welcomed by the Reverend and Mrs. Wilbur Parr. I had met her once years before, but I had forgotten. They gave me a key to their apartment, and I was free to come and go as I chose. They expected me at morning and evening meals. One day, the mailman brought a letter for me from Mrs. Parr's sister in Illinois. It had $10 in it to use for more sightseeing.

I saw much of New York by bus. I saw the United Nations headquarters, St. Bartholomew's Church, St. Patrick's Cathedral, and the Little Church Around the Corner. I rode the Staten Island Ferry to

St. John's Cathedral and saw the Statue of Liberty in the harbor. I also located the airport so I would know how to get there. My hosts took me to dinner on Sunday, and then to places they particularily wanted me to see. We crossed the Triborough Bridge into Queens, saw the Verrazano Narrows Bridge, Brooklyn Bridge, and Manhattan. It was a big contrast to the days when I rode a bicycle over the short dusty streets of Cooksville, Illinois, to see what I could see.

The morning of my flight arrived. My scripture was Psalm 139:1-9. In part it read, *"If I take the wings of the morning."* The Parrs took me to the bus that would get me to the airport.

CHAPTER TWO

Germany-Austria

"A man that hath friends, must show himself friendly. . . ."
—*Proverbs 18:24 (KJV)*

After landing in Reykjavik, Iceland, we flew to Luxembourg where I exchanged some money and bought a railroad ticket. From there, the train went so fast that I failed to get off at Trier, and, without the language, I could not explain to the conductor. The way I looked at myself, I was getting a bad start.

A passenger I had seen on the plane was brought to translate for me. Because I owed additional fare and didn't have the right change, the conductor put some of his coins with mine and I was able to get the ticket to Koblenz. He also directed me to the Hotel Hohmann, where I got a place to stay. In a pretty, little room, snuggled beneath a lovely down comforter, I felt at last that I had arrived in Europe.

The next morning, I had a late breakfast of ham, eggs, tea and toast. It was more substantial than the continental breakfasts I encountered later.

My goal in Germany was Bonn and then Cologne. Had I not hitch-hiked before, I might have been discouraged as I surveyed the little cars that passed by already full. But, I figured since I got a ride out of Alaska in the winter, I could get one here. I found it awkward to stand on the left side of the road and use my left thumb. Worse than that, I disliked not knowing how to converse when I got a ride.

I would like to have talked with the young man who took me to Bad Godesberg. Instead, I looked at the countryside where farmers were plowing and to the Rhine River where the traffic was varied.

Sometimes I pointed at things I saw and then my driver nodded and smiled with me.

He must have thought I wanted public transportation, because, after about 70 miles, he took me to a depot. It was a distance from the highway, so to avoid confusion, I bought a ticket to Bonn and Cologne.

Because the tourist season had not started yet, there was no central location to inquire about pensions. On my own, I found a nice hotel and left my suitcase. I had noticed at the depot that some people spoke English, so I went back there to eat.

I knew it was proper for a woman to have an escort in public. Reluctantly, I asked a U.S. Air Force officer at a table where he sat waiting for friends, if he would order some soup or stew and allow me to eat at his table. I promised to be gone before his people came. He understood and when I left, he gave me his wife's address in England in case I needed a contact there.

I started for my hotel, but soon realized I didn't know the way back. I didn't even have a receipt or a business card with the name on it.

"Never panic," I told myself. I went back inside the depot where I viewed four identical doors, one exit on each side of the building. By turns, I looked out each of them, searching for something that looked familiar, I didn't recognize anything.

I figured it was time to pray, so I put in a fervent prayer. When I looked out a door again, I saw a building which I remembered coming around earlier. I retraced my steps and was soon back at the Hotel Breslauer Hof, a hotel I never forgot. Again, my bed was made up with a down coverlet. I lay in the soft, cozy billows and gave thanks to God as I read from Psalm 119, *"Thou hast dealt well with thy servant . . . more than thousands of silver and gold."*

In the morning, I went to a bank and changed $20 to German money. I also studied a map showing important places to see that had been marked for me the day before by a man at the depot.

The first place I went was to the Cologne Cathedral with its two towers reaching 512 feet into the sky. Our family had had a picture of it on our wall in Bloomington. I never expected to actually see it. The marble inside was cold and I thought I understood why the priests wore so many robes. The structure was so vast, I could not

The Roman Wall. The museum where I visited "prematurely" is on the other side. Cologne, Germany, April 9, 1964.

see all of it in the time I had allowed.

I paid for my room for another day and walked to see the Roman Wall, a landmark left by Caesar. When he built something, I reflected, it stayed built. A street ran under an archway in the wall, and a portcullis hung above. I imagined it clanging down to shut out enemy legions.

On a gate nearby was a sign that read MUSEUM. I saw a nice-looking man go through, and I followed him. Turning toward me, he said the place was not open to the public. Had he said it in German, I might have turned away, but he said it in American-English, and to me that was an invitation.

I asked if I could peep in. He was reluctant but questioned me if I knew anything about oriental art. I said I did not, but I could look at it. Helpless to get rid of me, he told me to follow him. Inside, he turned me over to the caretaker, from whom I learned much. He led me to a storage room with priceless antiques. They were being catalogued for a museum yet to be constructed.

There were Ming vases with dragons, and there was one piece decorated with what looked like the ram caught in the brambles from the story of Abraham. "How did Abraham's ram get into the collection?" I asked.

The caretaker looked straight at me and answered in disgust, "Don't you know that Abraham came from Ur of the Chaldees? Surely, you know that the wise men came from the East?"

Yes, the East! I was properly squelched, although at first the piece did look out of place to me among the oriental treasures as I knew them.

After the museum, I crossed a bridge to arrange a boat trip on the Rhine for the next day. Something gripped my heart as I walked toward the dock and viewed the bridges still heavily damaged from World War II. I had never seen the paths of war.

The next day I was on the Rhine. There were boats of all kinds, large and small tugs, barges, and children floating in inner tubes. Other tourists relaxed on a river steamer which was larger and more grand than the one I rode. However, the view I had was every bit as good.

Farmers were plowing with oxen, mules or tractors. There were beautiful, terraced vineyards. Women wearing dresses were forking barnyard litter from carts onto the fields. It was a unique picture of rural life. On the heights were castles, some crumbled, some with scars from the war, and some restored to loveliness beyond description.

The public address system on our boat delivered a travelogue in German, but a teenager, fluent in languages, on his way to meet his father in Bavaria, told the stories about the castles in whatever language the passengers requested.

For lunch I used my last German coins and bought a large potato salad which I ate on the deck. Then, when we landed at Mainz, I took a taxi in order to locate a hotel and had no money. I borrowed ten marks from a passenger going to the Hotel Schoffenhof, and, in addition, I got another overnight loan to pay for my room. Communication was difficult.

On the morning of April 11, my scripture reading was from Jeremiah 33:3, *"Call unto me and I will answer thee and show thee great and mighty things which thou knowest not.''* After breakfast I cashed a traveler's check and paid my bills.

Drawn by organ music, I walked to a church in the center of a square and went in. There was no congregation, just the organist. I sat, reflected, and worshipped alone.

Mainz is noted for the printing of the Gutenberg Bible. I followed a tour group, hoping to find the museum. When they took a count, they found me to be extra and I was excluded. Amused that I had gotten in on quite a bit of the tour, I was disappointed that I missed seeing the Gutenberg museum.

My friends in Germany, Beth and Maurice Leiser who had written me to come to Europe, were stationed at Heidelburg. I rode an interurban bus to a highway where I planned to get started hiking toward Heidelburg, but there was no place to stand. I solved the problem by taking a trolley to the Mannheim Junction. I walked beyond a woman hiker so that she could get the first ride.

My ride was with a black American soldier and his pretty German wife. The soldier was so glad to see someone from the U.S. that he took me directly to my friends' door.

Since I was their first visitor from home, the Leisers gave me a royal welcome. They stayed at their neighbor's overnight and let me sleep in their king-sized bed. The Lord showed me "great and mighty things" that day.

On Sunday morning, Beth took me to Henry Village Chapel while Maurice was on duty. When Maurice came back we had a late lunch and then went sightseeing along the Neckar River in their bright red Pontiac. There were four castles to see. At Hirschhorn Castle, we drank tea on the rampart and looked out over the city, countryside, and locks.

Beth and I walked down to a tiny church with upright crypts around the walls. We walked through narrow streets and tunnels and over bridges. Maurice met us below.

There was one view I especially wanted. That was from the Hotel Europa, a castle taken over by the Army of Occupation for the use of personnel during World War II. When we arrived, we were at a height that presented a breathtaking scene, and dinner was served in a room with inlaid paneling. The food was some of the finest I have ever eaten.

Hirschhorn Castle on Neckar River in Heidelberg, Germany, April 12, 1964. (Courtesy of Beth Leiser)

We drove back to Heidelburg Castle. The daylight was gone, but orange-colored floodlights glowed, giving the landscape an eerie effect. It was as if ancient times had reappeared. Only the lights of surrounding cities kept us in reality. I thought of Daniel 4:2,3, *"How great are His signs! and how mighty His wonders!"*

Beth and I toured the next day. Schwetzen Palace, according to notes in my diary, was "too ugly to go into, too beautiful to leave." That is the only way I can describe it.

On the scene in Heidelburg, Germany, April 12, 1964. (Courtesy of Beth Leiser)

Without intending to we got into a group on a guided tour and were permitted to stay with them. Beth described it as a "finch bird tour." I don't remember why. Inside a court was a large ornately decorated bird house. A carved eagle sat at the entrance. There was a huge fountain with sculptured birds at the top spitting water down into a pool at the bottom. Beyond a walled area was a mosque with a prayer room. There was a secluded bath with inlaid shells and pieces of sparkling quartz. We were fortunate to have been guided through this seemingly exclusive area.

At the end of my visit, Beth and Maurice passed me on to my friends Barbara and Lennie Tuttle at Heilbronn. Barbara grew up with my children and she had two letters waiting for me from two of my daughters. One was from Hazel in Spain, who included some pesetas and told me to use them when I went to visit her.

The Tuttles and I spent time catching up on the news. I had stayed at their home in the states while hitchhiking. So we had much to talk about. The time with Barbara was fun because she hitchhiked, too.

We toured Heilbronn and saw the clock with mobile figurines striking the hour and the tulips beginning to bloom. We had some interesting rides and saw some places I had longed to see. One day we went to a Bible class, and though I did not know the teacher, he was from my hometown in Oregon. Once, while Barbara had other things to do, I hitchhiked to see the great castle at Ludwigsburg about fifty miles away. I rode in a school bus returning from its run. The driver took me to the castle. I was not prepared for the immensity of the grounds and the great statuary. I took pictures being careful not to get anything that would embarrass the film developer. I could not walk over all of the grounds, so I looked as far as I could see. The traffic had picked up when I returned.

My next goal was Munich where Barbara had friends. She phoned them that I would arrive the next evening. Lennie thought I would have no trouble hitchhiking the 250 miles there, because hiking was common.

I left my friends at 8 a.m. and started south on an assignment. I had promised a friend back home that I would send her a postcard from the TV tower at Stuttgart. I got the card and was in the tower by 9:30 a.m. The elevator operator told me on the way up that he had been in a U.S. prison camp at Ogden, Utah, during the war, and wished he were back in the U.S.

Down on the ground again, I met an American soldier with his wife and baby. They knew Beth and Maurice Leiser and offered to take me to Munich. They went out of their way to show me points of interest. We left the autobahn at Ulm, which is the birthplace of Albert Einstein. There we saw the Münster Cathedral with a tower 528 feet tall, the tallest church tower in the world. The couple especially wanted to see the furnaces at Dachau, but while they looked, I chose rather to view the park around the crematorium, the brilliant flowers, and the silent altar inside the monument. But all of the beauty would not blot out the memories of the gruesome acts that took place there.

We separated at the outskirts of Munich at two o'clock. A portion of scripture came to my mind from Exodus 14:13: *"Stand still and see the salvation of the Lord."* So I stood looking. I am sure I looked as irresolute as I felt. I had never met the people I was about to visit and didn't know how to locate the address Barbara had written out for me. After a series of misdirections and misunderstandings, the help of a girl on a bicycle, a woman who grabbed my suitcase to rush me to a waiting bus already tightly packed, and a young man who came along to help me untangle the mess I was in, I got onto the bus, the "Blue Goose," which took me into the correct neighborhood. When Barbara's friends met me, that ordeal was over.

I relaxed for the next few days, joining young wives of servicemen for hen parties. The interlude in Munich was fun, pleasant, and slow paced.

On the forty-fifth day of my tour, I began the morning with Pslam 31:24, *"Be of good courage, and He shall strengthen your heart, all ye that hope in the Lord."* The radio came on automatically, and the hymn "Sweet Hour of Prayer" was added to my devotions.

While I waited for my hosts to rise, I sorted letters, maps, and brochures, packing them to send home for safekeeping. I repacked my suitcase. After breakfast, I was on the road again.

A family on their way home gave me a ride, and we visited churches in Die Wies. We drove to a church 200 years old and sat there to hear the chimes in the old belfry ring out the noon hour. Then they located a pension for me where I could come and go as I pleased. The surroundings were beautiful with snow on the distant mountains and lovely spring flowers nearby. The stables adjoined the house. I retired after supper to my room. The moonlight streamed in my window. The Lord had truly "strengthened my heart."

Going on the next day, I visited Neuschwarstein Castle with its 200 rooms. I took a conducted tour and absorbed the history of that magnificent castle, built by slave labor. I learned that many artists had given their lives on the work before it was completed.

At Innsbruck, Austria, I met a couple who had a sister in the U.S. They helped me locate at the Hotel Roter Adler.

I learned from them that the American flag I had put on my suitcase to attract attention made me unpopular and was a detriment rather than a help to getting rides. I took it off. As I was waiting to get a ride out of Innsbruck, the cold wind nearly blew my hat off, and I had to tie it on with my scarf. By noon I was at Pettenau, and the next ride took me to Feldkirch. It was past time to eat, so I bought tea and cake at a neat little coffee shop.

During my next ride, I wondered if I was being given a ride or escorted. The driver was in uniform, and he slowed down at what probably was a boundary. He muttered to a guard something that sounded like "Damen." We were allowed to go through and went on to Liechtenstein.

After that, rides were scarce and the day became a real workout. I walked and walked. Two young boys on bicycles rode along beside me. Then, rather than riding, they got off their bikes and walked. They were very pleasant boys and even tried to get rides for me, even though we could not speak each other's language.

After two short rides, I walked some more. It was my day to walk. My verse that morning was Luke 9:43, " . . . *and they were all amazed at the mighty power of God."* I know I walked by "the mighty power of God." With such short rides, it was five o'clock when I reached Wallenstadt, Switzerland. I walked to the depot, the postcard shop, and to the tourist office.

CHAPTER THREE

Switzerland

"Let them shout for joy. . . . Let the Lord be magnified. . . ."
—*Psalm 35:27 (KJV)*

Wallenstadt is nestled in the mountains. Almost every home I saw was surrounded by flowers and an espaliered tree stood against the house wall. The tourist office was kept by a young woman who had a baby. Because it was closing time, the grandmother came to help take the baby home. Without benefit of a common language, they invited me to spend the night. I had fellowship in their home that didn't need words.

Switzerland was an important part of my European trip. When the Wyssen Skyline Cranes Co. Ltd. of Reichenbach, Switzerland, demonstrated skyline logging equipment in the Willamette National Forest area at Blue River, Oregon, I was nearby taking care of Prince and Marjorie Helfrich's home. I observed the equipment at work and became acquainted with some of the Swiss people who came along as a crew. Some still live at Blue River. Because of these connections, I had an awareness of Switzerland's beauty and I was anxious to experience the country.

My scripture the next morning was Psalm 34:15, *"The eyes of the Lord are upon the righteous, and his ears are open unto their cry."*

I was up early, writing cards and packing my suitcase. After the breakfast, an orange was added for me to take along. I took pictures of these ladies, Claire Lendi and her Mother Klara Bernold, with the baby, Theresa. They were such pleasant hostesses, I could not adequately express my gratitude.

It was 9:30 when I got to a hiking place to go toward Wadenswil where, by request, I was supposed to contact Richard and Emma Bader for John and Rosa Huber who lived in Eugene, Oregon. My first ride was in a Volkswagen station wagon. The driver spoke no English, but he understood where I wanted to go.

Seventy miles flew by. The scenery of lakes, rivers, towns, mountains and countrysides kept my eyes busy. I was let out at the depot where there was no language barrier, but there was a mix-up.

The depot agent made a phone call for me to Emma and Richard Bader. He was supposed to tell them that I was a friend of Rosa's, but he got the story crossed, and they understood that Rosa had come to see them.

The Baders were an older couple, and the Huber's had given me specific orders that I should not eat a meal there or trouble them by staying the night. It was heartbreaking to me when the Baders learned that I was not Rosa. I had only come to deliver a greeting. However, they could take things as they came, and that's the way they took me. Had I been their friend, they could not have treated me more kindly. Emma was so excited that she phoned a friend of hers who also knew the Hubers. In spite of my orders, there was much ado over my arrival. She fixed a lunch of Swiss "misen"—grated corn with cucumbers, rolls, and coffee, and we had a pleasant meal. But, there was more hospitality extended.

Emma had lived in Zurich, and my being there was an excuse to take the train to go back to see her city. We went, and it was a memorable place of beauty. Houses were built in keeping with the environment.

My hostess was a Christian, and the loving, pleasant association with her will never be forgotten. She even took me to a shoe repair shop to have new heel lifts put on my shoes. I had walked until they were worn down.

When we got back to Wadenswil, Robert had done his best to acquire the best Swiss cheeses known, an array that would make a connoisseur sit up and take notice. But it was wasted on me because I never learned to like cheese. I did my best to show appreciation; it was one of my most embarrassing moments. They also served little spuds cooked in their jackets, tasty breads and coffee.

The evening was spent keeping warm around a tiled stove made

Emma and Robert Bader in Wadenswil, Switzerland. (I visited April 21-22, 1964.)

by Matthew Stafen in 1782, and we talked about our mutual interests and friends. They also knew the Wyssen family in Reichenbach where I was going next. When we went to bed, we all could say, "The Lord is good."

Wednesday morning's scripture was Proverbs 3:23, 24, *"Then shalt thou walk in thy way safely, and thy foot shall not stumble. When thou liest down, thou shalt not be afraid; yea, thou shalt lie down, and thy sleep shall be sweet."*

I packed my things and folded the covers that I had slept under to help Emma with the extra work I had caused. After breakfast, I took a picture of the Baders to take back to Rosa and John.

Emma walked with me to a place where I could get a ride. A nice car came along, and I got in. We waved good-bye.

A second ride took me as far as Lucerne and the old wooden Chapel Bridge, popular with tourists. Black swans were swimming in the water below. It was not the season for the hanging baskets, and I regretted not getting to see them.

I walked to the highway going to Bern, the capitol. A city bus took me to the end of the line where I got a ride to Emmenbrücke, northwest of Lucerne. Then I had to walk again to get to the autobahn.

My next ride was with a man who was sightseeing and had field glasses. We stopped at points of interest I would not have seen otherwise. It was two o'clock when we parted at Trubschachen. Immediately, I was in another car. There was an offer of beer, which I refused. Six miles and I was in Langnau.

It was the usual walk to get from the center of town to the outer edge. On the way, I stopped at an ice cream company and ate a dish of ice cream. I realized that I was hollow as a gourd. My every fiber had absorbed the beauty of the country, but my stomach was empty.

A couple who picked me up spoke English and were unusually interested in me, what I was doing, and where I was going. They wanted my name and one of my newspaper clippings. It felt good to talk to someone, because I had been taking in and not giving out.

Before we got to Bern, I left them. Had there been someone like Emma waiting for me, I would have enjoyed it, but there was no thrill in the thought of being in Bern alone.

There was a coffee shop nearby where the couple left me. I had a Swiss pastry, bought some postcards and, then, because of road construction, I had to walk a distance to get a place to thumb a ride.

The next car took me 30 miles to Thun. To save time and guesswork, I took a bus about a five-mile distance to Guatt. According to my map, I would go to Spiez and from there get onto the highway to Reichenbach.

It was an older man who stopped for me. He did not speak fluent English, but he knew what I said when I told him I was going to Wyssen Skyline Cranes Co. at Reichenbach. I could understand that it was his destination also.

The man was stumbling for words to ask me why I was going to Wyssen's. He asked me again and again, because he could not understand what I said when I answered. How did I know these folks? He figured I was one of "those American women" or an American desperado, I guess.

The best I could do to clear myself was to show him Wyssen's name and phone number in my address book as well as the names of Jennine and Louis Constantin, Swiss people who lived in Blue River, Oregon. Louis had managed the Skyline logging for the Wyssen's there.

These were probably the only things that kept him from putting me out of the car. It was not until we arrived that I learned why he was so concerned.

There it was, a huge manufacturing plant covering several acres. On the hill above was the company's name formed by huge, dark green hedges, WYSSEN SKYLINE CRANES CO., LTD.

I suddenly felt faint. I was an interloper, as suspected. I had only seen these people a few times. Their friends in America had given me the address and phone number. What would these people think? We got out of the car. Quickly the driver stepped ahead of me into a building. When I went in, he stood between me and the man to whom he spoke, acting as a bodyguard, I was sure! I didn't need to know German to understand what was going on. I was thinking that I was about to be "ditched."

It was almost 5:30; I had nowhere to go for the night. I pointed to the telephone. I wanted them to call the Wyssen's, which they finally did.

A man made the call. Suddenly, his face took on a most surprised look. He was told, "Bring her out. We are expecting her!"

This was a favorable change, but how could they be expecting me. I didn't know when I would arrive there myself.

A man was delegated to take me to the Wyssen's home. The first driver left the scene in somewhat of a daze.

We pulled up to a lovely Swiss chalet. Around the house in the framing an inscription was carved which included the names of Jacob and Hannah Wyssen. According to the inscription, it was the desire of those who lived there that happiness would grow in the home from year to year as the rings grow in the trunk of a tree. Above and behind the house could be seen the peak of Neisen Mountain, snowcapped and beautiful.

I was greeted by Hannah as she held a letter out to me. It was from Emma Bader. That's how they knew I was coming. She was curious as to how far I travelled in the beautiful car I departed in when I left her. It was a mystery to me how it got there the same day I arrived, even though she went home and wrote it immediately.

It is incidents like this that kept me trusting in the Lord. I learned later that the Wyssen factory would ordinarily be closed at the time I arrived. I believe: "Things don't just happen, they are planned."

The Wyssen chalet in Reichenbach, Switzerland. Rain and fog prevented a good picture. (I arrived April 22 and left April 23, 1964.)

A place had already been set for me at the table, and I joined the family at their evening meal.

That night, there was a revival meeting at Adelboden, about 10 miles south of Reichenbach, and the family went in a caravan. I rode in a bus with the singers, eight girls who sang hymns in harmony all the way. Though I couldn't understand, the tunes were the same ones sung in America. The road wound through the Alps and the moonlight was as bright as day on the snow. There were varying shades of cold blue.

At the meeting, the singing and the setting were pure worship to me. The soloist sang in German-Swiss, "His Eye Is On the Sparrow." The last time through he sang the chorus in English. "For the guest," he said. When he sang the words: "And I know He watches me" I got chills all over. For me, the words were appropriate.

I picked out certain words and phrases from Pslam 111 the next morning as I wrote cards to send home. *"Praise . . . the works of the Lord are great . . . He hath given meat . . . praise!"*

The family was getting ready for school and work when I joined them for breakfast. Three of their four children were home. Hannah wanted to go with me when I got started, so I waited until she was ready. She drove me to Spiez and showed me the surrounding country to compare it with Oregon. There is a similarity. But nothing compares with the Alps.

I told her that I was apprehensive about hiking in Italy, and she insisted that I should see Venice.

At the depot, this darling woman personally had my Eurail Pass validated and provided me with all of the instructions needed for my ride. I felt like I belonged to Switzerland.

CHAPTER FOUR

Italy

"The Lord preserveth the strangers. . . ."
Psalm 146:9 (KJV)

In order to get my $130's worth out of my Eurail ticket, I had to start using it. I would rather have hitchhiked, so I could see the scenery.

The train crossed the continental divide into the fantastic Rhone River Valley. I showed my pass at Brig, Domodossada, and again at the Italian border. At Milan there was a layover between trains and a woman paid my way on a tram to see Milan's Duomo with her.

Back on Track #10, it seemed that everyone was going to Venice. I had a first-class seat, but for the next six hours a little boy traveling with his parents crawled back and forth across my feet.

The next morning, awaking in Venice's Terminal Hotel, I opened my eyes to darkness. The shutters had been closed and it was raining.

I went by boat to St. Mark's Square. Visibility was bad because the cabin windows were fogged. I went out on the deck near the wheelhouse in the rain. Tourists don't do that, so I was investigated by a man who thought I might be crazy, but I told him I just wanted to see.

The dreary day spoiled St. Mark's for me. I got breakfast and then boarded the train for Florence. There, I got a nice pension and took a bus to Michelangelo Hill. The view of the white marble city was breathtaking. I thought of Emma again and how pleasant it would have been to have her enjoy the scene with me.

I decided not to go to Rome and several other noted places I had read about because I didn't want to go alone, and my scripture didn't give me a "go" sign. It was April 25, and Hazel said I should be in Zaragoza before May 1st. I scheduled my tours accordingly.

There was a 9:45 train the next morning to Pisa. In the interval, I studied the architecture of the Cupola de Brunelleschi. It appeared to me that man had put more emphasis on the temporal than the spiritual. It was different than any I had seen.

Crowded into a train compartment, I wished I was hitchhiking. An English-speaking lieutenant colonel in the Italian Navy made it almost pleasant as he told me about the countryside seen only as it flashed by.

My goal was the Leaning Tower. As soon as the train stopped, I flew to a locker and stored my suitcase. A horse-drawn cab, called a phaeton, was in a hurry to leave and took me to the foot of the Tower where a massive procession was forming. It was an annual event.

Standards with various insignia were held high. There were black Christos and ornate, glittering crucifixes. Floats bearing images shown with ornaments and pomp. It was scintillating, moving pageantry. I could not have seen the Leaning Tower at a more spectacular time, and the phaeton driver had hurried to get me there.

As time was getting away, I signaled my driver to move out ahead of the crowd. As the horse clip-clopped back to the depot, I praised the Lord for the beauty of spring along the Arno River.

From our compartment, the lieutenant colonel continued to point out historical places along the Mediterranean Coast. He left the train in Northern Italy.

Wise council came from a Spanish family who spoke English. They were getting off the train in Italy to spend the night rather than go into France where it was more expensive. It was to my advantage to get off too, because I wanted to see Monaco, Cannes and the French Riviera in daylight.

At the border, my passport was stamped, and as I prepared to leave, I was told in several languages that I was not allowed to get off the train. "Can't" always meant "can" to me and my old nature took over. When the train stopped at the siding for customs, I grabbed my suitcase and got off. Quickly, I went to the sidewalks under the tracks. I was in Ventimiglia, a border city.

I inquired about the morning train and the agent said 9:30. But, at my hotel, the manager said 7:15. He was allowing time to go through customs, but my passport had already been stamped.

My last Italian coins were spent on a peach truffle that served as my supper.

I awoke at 5:30, and realizing my state of affairs, I committed my way to the Lord. I had no idea how I would get past customs.

At the station, I bravely inquired about the departure time for Barcelona, Spain. Two customs officers overheard me speaking American-English and came toward me. I watched them in their colorful, tailored outfits. When they were directly in front of me, I thought, "Now, here it comes."

"Lady, please tell us what 'Go twirl your baton' means." Their manner was respectful, and the absurd request stunned me.

When I got myself together I grinned, "It means, in effect, to go mind your own business."

They were so grateful to me that they went with me past customs and helped me onto the train, never knowing how much I needed them. It was time to praise.

As we traveled along the coast of France, it was with ecstasy that I viewed the sunlight shining brightly on the roses and wisteria in full bloom, the homes perched on hillsides, and palm trees lining the white, sandy coastline of the blue Mediterranean. Monte Carlo was a picturebook city, more like fantasy than reality.

Along the route, we stopped to let on more passengers. I watched. Boys who were about 12 years old, dressed uniformily in red shirts and blue jeans and followed by a priest, boarded the train. Following a discreet distance behind her husband, a lady from India, draped in native costume and wearing a diamond in her nose, mounted the steps. A black man who spoke English sat down beside me and provided interesting information about the places we passed. Houses were made of stone, and there were gardens, vineyards, oil distilleries, and gorgeous bright flowers flashing by.

The train switched engines at a big stone fort and at Port-Bou, the border town, we were herded like cattle to show our tickets and then our passports. The process was repeated in order to board the train for Spain.

CHAPTER FIVE

Spain

Thou shalt not be afraid for the terror by night,
nor for the arrow that flieth by day.''
—Psalm 91:5 (KJV)

It was 11 o'clock at night when we arrived in Barcelona, Spain. I turned down the offer of a shabby-looking man who wanted to walk me to a pension. I asked a policeman about a hotel. He muttered, "Marina," and walked away.

I could see I needed help. I prayed and the Lord helped me. A young Australian girl who was waiting for her parents outside of a tavern spoke English and helped me locate the Hotel Marina. She walked with me, then returned to her post to wait.

In the morning, I calculated that I still had 300 miles to go to get to my daughter in Zaragoza. When I went to pay my hotel bill, I didn't have the right change. Neither a five-dollar bill nor a traveler's check would do. They insisted on keeping my suitcase, camera and coat for security while I went to the bank, but the bank wasn't open yet. Then I remembered the pesetas my daughter had sent to me in Heilbronn. I was able to pay my bill and redeem my belongings.

The train didn't leave the depot until noon, so I watched the activity that went on nearby. Street sweepers were cleaning with push brooms and putting trash into hand-woven baskets. Handcarts, similar to the ones used in American cities, were being pushed, and like an echo from the past, I imagined the men were calling, "Any rags, any bones, any bottles today?"

On the way again, I observed the Elbe River sullen and muddy yellow. We passed Roman forts, private homes and more vineyards. At last we were at the Zaragoza depot.

I phoned Hazel to meet me. When she came I was so excited I almost cried, but I wouldn't let myself. She took me to Hostel de Oroel where she had reserved a room for me. I expected this because I knew there was not any extra space in their tiny apartment at the Zaragoza Air Force base where my son-in-law was stationed. Besides, one does not absorb the flavor of an area by staying on an American base.

Hazel took me to several places in the days I was there. One was a delightful, sorely needed, trip to a beauty shop. We went to an open-air market that opened twice a week. There were many kinds of colorful, fresh vegetables, but pretty as they were, they had to be purified in Clorox before they were safe to eat. The meat displayed in the open air drew flies.

We had a trip to a Jesuit monastery with members of a woman's organization. What impressed me there was that after many wars and five eras of remodeling, it had become a conglomeration of architectural styles. Only the alabaster windows were unchanged.

One morning I went by myself to a church service. There I met a man who said he had turned down an offer to teach school in my home town, Eugene, Oregon. I got back to Hostel de Oroel by taking a taxi. I was back before Hazel came to get me.

The day I left Zaragoza, Hazel gave me more money. I arrived at 10:00 p.m. in Madrid. It was the day before the May Day fiesta. There was activity everywhere when the taxi let me out in front of a hotel. It was on an awful, alley-like street and it was dark.

Fellow travelers had given me the address, but they had misjudged me. My verse in the morning was from Ezekiel: ''Ye shall live.'' I was having second thoughts; my knees were wobbly.

The taxi driver indicated a door. As I approached, a man came out of the crowd, took out a big ring of keys, and unlocked it. He let me in and turned on the light. When I got beyond the door a ways, he turned out the light, went out, and locked the door behind him. I was locked in and I had to get out. Just before the light went out, I caught a glimpse of an empty room ahead of me. There was also a hallway that led upstairs where a dim light revealed a hall.

As I approached the stairway, I heard the voices of both men and women above in revelry. I dared to knock on a slightly opened door where I was met by an unfriendly stare. It was with great effort that I made my wishes known. I was escorted rudely down the stairs. The door was unlocked and I was put outside. Things got more complicated when I again showed the address to a man in the crowd. I was led up another flight of stairs, this time on the outside of a building. In another room, I was shown a book of names of American men. I was supposed to choose a "blind date." But I wasn't looking for a date, and when they understood, they took me to the door.

Outside, it was like the crowd focused on me. A little boy was picked out and sent on an errand. When he came back, the man with the keys gave my suitcase to him and had him take me to a decent hotel.

Bright daylight woke me. My scripture was from Jeremiah, *"Fear thou not . . . be not dismayed . . . I am with thee."* It was my assurance.

Folks in the States had encouraged me to see Seville. The Talgo was the only train, and it was scheduled to leave at 1:25 p.m. With my spare time, I decided to see more of Madrid before my train left. I tried to make the descriptions given to me of the city fit what I saw, but I could not. After the night before, my eyes were not seeing a "majestic city." I was glad to board the train.

The trip south to Seville was through farmlands and vineyards. We went through many tunnels. It was 10:30 p.m. when we arrived. May celebrations were going on there, too.

I tried to keep out of trouble this time. I asked some ladies to recommend a good hotel. A redcap took me to the Hotel Francio, where I got a room with a bath and was able to bring myself and belongings up to standard. Even though it was noisy outside, iron shutters on the windows kept out the sounds of motorcycle racing, shouts, and drunken laughter. I had no trouble going to sleep, but I never felt completely at ease alone in Spain.

The next day I tried a new method of sightseeing; I hired a taxi to take me places. I went to castles, to a cathedral where chanting resounded from a vaulted ceiling, and to the American Plaza where there were mosaics and tiles in tiny detail. I rode through a huge park with palm trees and gorgeous flower beds.

At the depot, I met an Air Force man who was about to be transferred to Mountain Home, Idaho, after three years of overseas duty.

He was returning to Madrid, having shipped his car from Cadiz to the states. We both had time on our hands, and I asked him to go with me to see more of Seville. He was happy to do so, and we hired another taxi.

It was again night-time when the train returned to Madrid. This time I got a taxi to take me to the Castellana Hilton. I still had $100 in traveler's checks and felt flush. However, I didn't take a very expensive room. What mattered most was that I knew what I was doing.

The next morning was Sunday, and I went by taxi to a Church of England sanctuary, a remodeled castle. I ate at a neighborhood restaurant, and then had the owners call a taxi to take me to the depot. I was taking no chances.

My next destination was Bilbao. I had met Basque people in Eastern Oregon, and I wanted to see the region from which they came.

It was a full day's trip, and there were no compartments on the train for me to hole up in. A Dutchman who rode with me was astonished to see an American woman who didn't smoke or drink and who liked to look at the scenery.

The hillsides were terraced and under cultivation. Oxen, as they plowed, carried yokes on their horns. The yokes were covered with huge sheepskin pads that made them look like hats. They were shades from the sun.

Again, it was night-time when the train arrived. A young Basque navy man referred me to the Arana Hotel in Bilbao. I felt a surge of confidence, but found on my arrival that there was no vacancy. It was the same at the next hotel: "Complete." It was said in such a way that I felt I must be doing something wrong again. I almost threw myself under a taxi to stop it so the driver would take me to a hotel. He made it plain, in English, what he thought about a woman alone on the streets at night. Muttering things unknown to me, he took me to a nice hotel. Under his escort, I had no problem getting a room, but I realized I was fortunate whenever I got a taxi or a room without an escort. I registered at the Excelsior, where English was spoken.

Heading for France, I was sure I didn't have enough of the right money for a ticket. No one would cash a traveler's check at the depot, and I could find no one who spoke English. I prayed as I walked to the ticket window where I pointed to my map and poured out all my coins. There were francs from France, Italian lira, and various other coins. The man behind the counter laughed. He shoved all of them back at me except one little insignificant-looking one and said in English, "Third class, Number 2." To my surprise, he gave me change from the little coin. I had been concerned for no reason.

CHAPTER SIX

France and Belgium

*"Lord, my heart is not haughty, nor my eyes lofty, neither do I
exercise myself in great matters or things too high for me."*
—Psalm 131:1 (KJV)

My Eurail Pass put me in a first class compartment with a fine,
well-educated French couple, both of whom were blind. I was impressed with the blessing of having sight. When I went to dine, there
was no table empty. I went back to my seat, and the couple knew
that I had not gotten any food. They gave me two oranges and a
cookie.

It was late when we arrived in Paris. I tried to go to the Hotel Lor-
raine, a place the blind couple had told me about, but it was the
same story as in Spain. I needed an escort. I tried for a taxi again,
but what the driver said in French, I guessed, was worse than I heard
in Spain. I finally got a driver who took me to Hotel Paris Maube-
hauge, but he told the desk clerk all sorts of things about "bad
characters" like me. I was too tired to care.

The next day a change of dress, a scripture verse, and a breakfast
of coffee, milk, and a roll helped me to start things anew.

It has always been my opinion that the best way to see a place
is from a height. I took a bus to the Eiffel Tower. My heart filled with
praise as I gazed from its height on the panorama below. As I stood
looking, I was approached by a young lady and her boyfriend. She
asked, "Are you Mrs. Small from Eugene, Oregon?" When I got my
breath, I told them I was. The girl was an American going to school
in Germany. Her uncle had sent her the news clipping from the

On May 5, 1964 I met people in this tower from Eugene, Oregon who recognized me. (Souvenir postcard)

Eugene Register-Guard. It had my photo and her uncle had said she should watch for me. At that moment, the world seemed small, and it kept getting smaller before I left the tower.

At another viewpoint, I met three young men from Eugene. We discussed the problems that arise when one knows only one language.

As I started down, I met two U.S. Army men from Heilbronn, Germany. It turned out that I knew their sergeant. What surprised me more was their question, "Say, you wouldn't be the old lady mentioned on the radio the other day who was hitchhiking?" I admitted it, but after all I had been through with taxi drivers, I was afraid to ask what was said about me. It occurred to me that the couple who had interviewed me previously in Langnau, Switzerland, were, no doubt, responsible.

A boat ride on the river was a wonderful way to sightsee, too. A French girl announced the landmarks in English over a loudspeaker as we glided down the Seine. To see more of the city, I walked, making use of my city map to locate historical points. I stared at the Arc de Triumphe until I was bugeyed.

I had tried for several days to contact friends from Eugene, Jim and Beverly Burroughs. They were missionaries and lived a little way outside Paris. It was a Wednesday when I finally got in touch with them.

A tourist hostess explained that my Eurail Pass should get me to their town, but she left out one essential detail, a transfer. I took the route she told me but failed to get the transfer ticket at the end of the line to show at a turnstile entrance. When I started through I was stopped. It appeared that I was trying to "gyp" the railroad.

A cocky little uniformed woman, displaying her power, ordered me to follow her as if I were in custody. Playing the part, I walked as meekly as I could behind her, trying to keep my laughter bottled up. A soldier could not have marched more ceremoniously than she did, nor a prisoner more humbly.

When she brought me into the inquiry room, she stood at attention until my case was brought before the judge. I looked at an agent nearby who gave me a wink as if to say he had seen the woman perform before. The judge took my Eurail Pass, looked at it and handed it back to me, announcing its validity. In the tone people use to correct a toddler, he told the woman to escort me through the turn-stile and over the bridge into the town where I wanted to go.

Outside the iron gates of the courtyard at my friends, I called loud-ly for a drink of water while I rang the bell. The Burroughs family of seven came running with four ducks, a black dog and a cat trail-ing behind. They knew my voice, and I really did want a drink of water. What a welcome!

I enjoyed my time with Jim and Beverly and their children, Jim-my, Rosemary, Stephen, David and Evangeline. My invitation had come many years before. The next day was a holiday, Ascension Day. The family slept in, but I was up early and read Romans 8:28, *". . . we know that all things work together for good to them that love God. . . ."*

At the Baptist church we sat together. The messages were in French, and I caught a few words I could understand. It was an all-day session from 10:00 a.m. on, so I was glad when we got back home. I left the next morning for Belgium.

In Brussels, I met a young man from New Jersey at a tourist in-formation counter. Like me, he had little money to spend, but wanted to see the city. The woman in the booth suggested that we take the streetcar to the World's Fair grounds. The young man, Stanley J. Wartens, became my tour companion that day. We climbed the Atomium and got an overall view of the city. From this overgrown "Tinker Toy," we saw how groups of plants of different colors were arranged below to make a picture of the city of Brussels. I was pleased with the view even though the climb had made me tired. It was up, up and up. When we parted, Stanley gave me his card and asked me to write when I got back to Oregon.

I went to St. Catherine Tower and the Church of St. John the Bap-tist at the convent. I had anticipated a well-kept place, but there were souvenir booths outside which hid much of the beauty and dirt and clutter inside.

The next day, I went to Louvain. The trip was about 30 miles by train. I taxied from the depot to the town hall, which is an enor-mous stone building. Each of the stones had the name of an American town or school carved on it. I learned that during World War II, the building had been destroyed by bombs. American school children had donated money for the inscribed stone blocks which had restored it.

The Atomium in Brussels, Belgium, May 8, 1964.
(Souvenir postcard)

About that time an English lady with her daughter, a nun, came along and invited me to go with them to a stone cathedral where the nun taught.

There were many beautiful wood carvings in the cathedral. One hand-carved tree spread its branches to form a canopy over the pulpit. Another carving depicted a horse throwing its rider. I wondered what the horse was doing in church. The sister looked at me as if I were a heathen. She asked, "Didn't you ever hear of Paul being struck blind on the way to Damascus?" Well, I never envisioned him on a horse, but she assured me that "Of course, he would be riding a horse!" While I didn't agree, I let the matter rest.

Train time to Mechelen was at noon. I thanked the women and

hurried to board. Two English-speaking men on the train advised me to be sure to see the carillons for which the city was famous.

It was a memorable experience. I could not absorb the greatness of these carillon bells at St. Nombout. There I saw another carving of Paul being thrown from a horse. At St. John's Church, there were famous paintings by Van Dyck and Rubens.

Belgium was, to me, the most foreign of all the countries I visited. The people were friendly, but of all places visited, I was most conscious there of being a stranger.

CHAPTER SEVEN

Netherlands and Denmark

". . . doing the will of God from the heart."
—Ephesians 6:6 (KJV)

Going into Holland, we passed through Antwerp, Belgium, and then into the Dutch cities of Rotterdam to Leiden.

A tourist inn was suggested to me and when I got a room it was as small as a closet. The bed let down from the wall, and there was only one blanket. I had to use my coat to keep warm. In the night, a drunk staggered part way into my room and, apologizing, backed out as quickly as he could. I put my suitcase against the door to hinder any further intrusions.

It rained in the night, but I was too tired to notice that the roof was leaking. Part of my bed got wet. My scripture was from Isaiah 30:18-21 the next morning, *"Wait, that He may be gracious unto you . . . wait, He will answer . . . this is the way, walk ye in it."*

I was repaid for the inconveniences by the landlady who fixed me a good breakfast. I had not been eating well and I was losing weight. I was also getting a cold and the damp room did not help any.

I left my suitcase at the depot and set out to sightsee as usual. I visited the Plymouth Church where the Pilgrims were incited to go to America. An English-speaking usher showed me the alms houses and historical plaques. One of my best friend's great-grandfather had been a pastor there. She told me that the crypts in the floor had been marred by the spike heels of women's shoes. The scars had been sanded down, so some of the names of the crypts were illegible.

The pews had doors on them, and families rented them. I found a vacant one and sat in it for the service. For some reason, I was "passed the hat" three times. I guess I didn't give what I was supposed to the first two times. The sermon was in Dutch and an hour long. There was no heat, and the stone structure was damp and cold. I was glad when I got out into the sunshine.

Picking up my suitcase, I took the train to see the tulips. I found Keukenhof Garden beautifully landscaped and filled with brilliant color. The blocks of gorgeous flowers, bathed with bright sunlight, were dazzling. Ducks and ducklings swam in a tree-lined creek. There were greenhouses, a windmill, and paths winding through the lawn. The place was so large that I had to leave acres and acres of beauty behind me, unseen for lack of time.

By Eurail, I traveled to Haarlem where I got a train to go to Puttgarten in Germany. By this time, my cold was getting worse. I felt so bad that I wasn't thinking clearly and got off the train before my stop. But another train came along to take me to my destination. On the second train, there was room to stretch out, although I couldn't sleep.

It was a beautiful, grand morning when our coach was loaded on the ferry to cross the Baltic Sea between Germany and Denmark. I went on deck to scan the horizon, drink coffee, and read in my New Testament about Paul. But, I could not find anything about him falling off a horse.

The tourist agency at Copenhagen, Denmark, directed me to a nearby hotel where I spent the night. I also slept in the next day and paid for another night. I was exhaused. On the following day, I paid the rest of my bill. They charged me for food I didn't eat and for polishing my shoes, which they hadn't done. I paid it without question. I got breakfast before I left.

I contacted friends in Suserup, who came and picked me up. I had met Kej Nielsen in Eugene, and at this time I met his wife, Bodel, who spoke no English. They had two small children and were a Christian family. They gave me a wonderful time.

Their stone house had a thatched roof—a kind of roof I especially wanted to see—over 100 years old. It had a lovely, landscaped courtyard and there were several smaller stone storage buildings set back from the house.

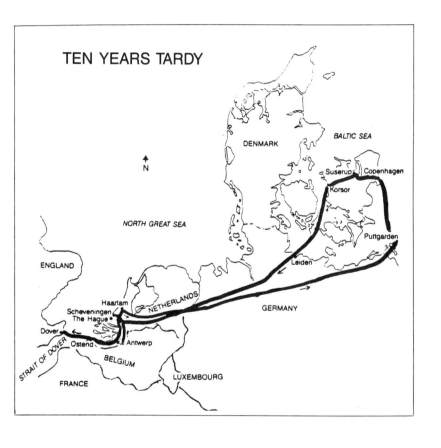

A drive after dinner took us through rolling farmlands with old houses that were very well cared for. The surrounding land looked "loved," as I saw it.

With Kej and Bodel, I learned the meaning of the word vestibule. We were visiting a twelfth century church where the entrance was almost as large as the auditorium. In ancient times, when warriors came to worship, they removed their mail and vestments and laid down their armor, crossbows, shields and swords before they entered to worship. The anteroom, called a vestibule, had to be large enough to hold it all.

The Nielsens' house was in turmoil on this day. Carpenters had come to put down a new floor, and an electrician came to repair the stove. The rest of the uproar was about me. A reporter and photographer came to do an interview and take my picture. They stayed for coffee. An article was published in a leading Danish newspaper on May 29. The headline read, "Great-Grandmother Hitchhikes All the Way from Oregon to Suserup." The article said, "Wonderful 68-year-old American lady responds to a ten-year-old invitation on her thumb." My picture was taken beside a sign that pointed the way to the old church we had visited.

The family sang gospel songs my last evening there, while Bodel played the piano. Though the songs were in Danish, I knew the tunes, and the harmony was beautiful.

When I left, Kej put me on the train at Korsor. The train took me back to the steamship dock. During the steamship crossing, a young pencil salesman, Martin Martens, bought me a cup of coffee. He was with me at the next train depot and led me to my car, thus helping me to bypass the language barrier. I welcomed this kind of assistance.

The train crossed the border between Germany and the Netherlands, and when it arrived at The Hague, a friendly couple insisted that I go home with them because it was so late. After a good night's rest and a bountiful breakfast, they took me to a bus depot and handed me a ticket to Scheveningen, a port city not far away. This was unexpected hospitality, and I regret I do not have their names.

I planned for the days ahead. My Eurail Pass and my money were about used up so I decided to see several of the places nearby and wrote off seeing more of France. Then, I would cross the English Channel to Dover.

CHAPTER EIGHT

To England

". . . Stand ye in the ways . . . ask for the old paths . . .
walk therein, and ye shall find rest for your souls. . . ."
— Jeremiah 6:16 (KJV)

I left for England with the promise of Isaiah 58:11: *"The Lord shall guide thee continually, and satisfy thy soul. . . ."*

I found good traveling companions to Ostende, Belgium, where a boat was waiting. Crossing the Strait of Dover was smooth, and three young athletes sat near me on deck. Two decided to walk around, leaving the third, who had an injured foot. He looked forlorn, and it was natural for me to offer myself as a sounding board. The three had been to Ostende for a racing elimination contest. This young man had slipped and torn a tendon.

His car was at Dover, and he invited me to ride with them to Nottingham, where they lived. When we docked, one of his friends had to drive his car, and I shall never forget the ride. While it was right to drive on the left side of the road, I never got used to it. The owner of the car, used to being in command, "drove" from the back seat. When we got into the residential and shopping districts of London, it became obvious that they were lost.

"Now I know where I am. Turn left!" said the car owner. In a little while, he remarked, "This looks familiar. Turn left." When it was time for another decision, the young man at the wheel asked, "What do I do now?" The answer came from the back seat, "I don't know this place. Turn left."

By this time, it wasn't funny. I knew that if you turn left every time, you eventually come back to your starting place. The driver had taken so many left turns, he said smoke was coming out of his ears. I figured that since there was "smoke," there would be fireworks, and I didn't want to stay for it. I had them to let me out.

I asked a policewoman about a place to stay for the night. She went with me a few blocks to rows of adjoining houses. They were bed and breakfast houses. "The windows will have signs in them to advertise vacancies," she said.

I found a room, but the landlady wouldn't cash a traveler's check. She said she would hold my passport for the night as security.

It was 7 p.m. and I had missed two meals. On my way, I had bought a sweet cake at a bakery and a banana at a huckster's wagon. They held me through until morning.

Cornflakes, bacon, eggs, coffee and rolls were pleasantly served for my breakfast. I explained to the landlady that I needed my passport to cash a traveler's check at the bank. She was willing to accept my suitcase, camera and two coats in exchange. I cashed my last two traveler's checks, paid my bill and got back my possessions. The total cash left to get me back to Oregon was $16.

I was somewhere in London, but I had no idea where. I got a map at a nearby garage. The attendant suggested that I should transfer my air ticket to Glasgow, Scotland. I had been scheduled to leave from Luxembourg. He telephoned the Icelandic Airlines office to see if the switch could be made. It could, and I went to the office to make a change. There were several days remaining before my scheduled flight.

I didn't know how to get out of London and asked a city bus driver. He didn't know either. During the course of the conversation, I mentioned that my ancestors were British, and one of my mother's given name was Richmond. He laughed and pointed, saying, "Lady, that bus over there goes to Richmond."

I took the bus and went to Richmond. But I had gone south and needed to go north toward Scotland. I felt rewarded, however, because the ride took me through Hampton Court. I walked around looking at the flower gardens. Each planting was a showpiece. The palace, built in 1732, had been beautifully cared for through the centuries.

I stayed that night in the Angel Hotel. It cost more than I should have paid with my limited resources, but it was so very old English that I couldn't resist. My room had slanted ceilings, and the plastered walls, with irregular timbers, were Elizabethan and dated back to 1633.

The next morning, I asked the Lord to guide me. Scotland was my destination, and moneywise I was through with trains or buses. I put up my thumb. The first ride was short.

On my second ride, the young driver took me to see Arundel Castle. Following that, rides were numerous. There were many kindnesses shown to me. I was taken on tours that I could not afford. One young man, John E. Hamlen, took me to Chichester to see some artistically designed stone houses. He took me to see the home of the Earl of Richmond because I had told him how I had tried to leave London by using Richmond, my mother's given name. He also took me to dinner at a fine old restaurant.

The next ride took me through Portsmouth, where we drove past seagoing vessels and ruined castles with swans swimming in the moats.

In Salisbury, the Inquiry Room directed me to the home of a Mrs. Pink, where I spent the night.

A cup of tea served in bed started the morning. There were cathedrals to see, and I planned to inquire about Stonehenge. I had seen the replica in the state of Washington on the Columbia River and wanted to see the original. When I asked about it at a store, the owner brought me a newspaper to show me a current news article. One of Stonehenge's 25-ton monoliths had fallen, and the picture showed a huge crane lifting it back into place. The man gave me the article, and I cherished it for my album.

Salisbury Cathedral was not to be overlooked. It is English architecture built in the thirteenth century and was a marvel to me. I viewed its stately 404-foot spire, the second-highest in the world.

As I walked toward Stonehenge, I came upon a man and his wife working in their tulip garden. I set my suitcase down and asked, "Is this the road to Stonehenge?"

The man answered, "Yes, Ma'am, but it is 12 miles. Lady, you can't walk it."

I said, "Thank you, but it is much closer than it was in Oregon." I walked on.

Soon I heard someone running behind me. Gasping and panting, the man caught up with me. "Madam, my wife told me to take you to Stonehenge." This was welcome news, because I had not seen one car on the road.

Mr. C. P. Wood, his wife beside him, drove along the Avon River, and I was their passenger in the back seat. We were on a very old, straight, level road built by the Romans. Mrs. Wood brought a hot, fresh bun in a paper sack for me to eat on the way. When we arrived, Mr. Wood paid my entrance fee. I thanked them enthusiastically. I wrote to them the next Christmas because I was so grateful for the ride and their kindness.

The big derrick used to raise the monolith was a sharp contrast to the prehistoric setting. People were there from all over the world. The Summer Solstice was approaching, and movie companies were setting up. Archaeologists were digging and sifting. Children were climbing and running.

Wondering how those huge stones were transported and set up with such perfect precision gave an old rock gardener like me a lot of respect for the ancient builders. After soaking up the atmosphere for some time, I turned once more toward Scotland.

One driver, an English army lieutenant, took me to see Wells Cathedral and bought pictures for me of the charming medieval church with its tower, chapel, cloisters, and magnificent statuary. When we left, he insited that I take a five-pound note. We exchanged addresses, and at Christmas time, he wrote me that he had become a major.

I walked along by the Lord Mayor's Castle watching the swans. At the edge of town, I got a ride to Bath. The driver let me out at the cathedral with its fan-shaped ceilings and stained-glass windows. I didn't have enough money to see the Roman Baths. At four o'clock, I decided to try for one more ride before dark.

The driver of a car which was parked beside the road figured I was a hitchhiker. He said his wife was shopping, and when she came back they would take me to their home. When she came, she added her invitation to his. They were Mr. and Mrs. G. E. Davies. Their last child had left home, and they were lonesome.

Their home was built on an old Roman structure. It had walls three feet thick and was surrounded by a wall with iron gates. When I said the blessing at the dinner table, they confessed that they had been neglecting to read their Bibles and to pray.

(At Christmas time they wrote a letter to ask me to pray for their married daughter, mother of three children, who faced a serious operation. They never sent the letter. Before they could mail it, the daughter died, and the letter I received told of her death. The daughter had married into royalty, and the couple didn't know if they would be allowed to visit their grandchildren. I prayed for them, remembering that I had slept in that daughter's room the night I stayed there.)

When I left the next day, the Davies drove me to see the Roman Baths that I thought I would never get to see, and they paid my way. When we parted, Mr. Davies also insisted that I take a five-pound note. I never felt right about it, and I reimbursed them at Christmas.

The next night, I was exhausted from traveling. I got a room in Gloucester. The landlady had a daughter in the United States in Renton, Washington. She invited me to sit before a cheery fire and talk with the family. She heated water for me to freshen up before I went to bed, and I knew, as sleep came easily, that the Lord had taken care of me again. In the morning, the woman prepared an excellent breakfast. I walked to Gloucester Cathedral for Sunday services.

I proceeded northward, through Stratford-on-Avon to Nottingham and found a bed and breakfast house for the night. By the time I got settled and went out to eat, everything was closed. I went hungry until morning. I had lost much weight from going without meals, and my clothes were not fitting anymore.

Breakfast was a satisfying one with ham, eggs, cereal, tea, and even baked beans. I walked up the hill to Nottingham Castle with an anxious step. I couldn't afford the admission fee. The best I could do was peep in the windows. Outside, I enjoyed the statues of the characters from *Robin Hood* and found the view from the hill spectacular.

CHAPTER NINE

Scotland

"Because he hath set his love upon me,
therefore will I deliver him. . . ."
—Psalm 91:14 (KJV)

Going toward York my thumb stopped the driver of a furniture lorry who was glad to have my company. I found his stops fascinating. He took two expensive chairs to a remodeled carriage house, and made another delivery to a restored castle adding to its priceless furnishings. At Perry Bridge he bought our dinner with entrees of roast beef and Yorkshire pudding. "Everyone who comes to Yorkshire must have Yorkshire pudding," he said.

After the meal, he took me on a tour of the city. Wherever the lorry could fit through the narrow gates of the turreted Roman stone walls, we went. I was thankful to be a hitchhiker and not a tourist on a group tour. I could never have had such a good time.

After getting a room on Exhibit Square, I made a special effort to go to the Central Records Office and search out our family name. I learned that they were cabinet makers while other men worked in the coal mines. I walked to see the Monk's Gate and York Minster, England's largest cathedral. I took time to sit on a bench and enjoy the magnificent stained-glass windows.

Two young men walked by and as they talked, I could tell where they were from. I called, "Hello, Iowa." They came over and I learned they were driving to Scotland. I could go along if I managed my own expenses.

I pointed out my room so they could come to get me in the morning and continued my tour.

My skinny self at the doorway of "Monk Bar" on the Wall of York, Yorkshire, England, May 25, 1964. Taken by Edwin L. Roswell III.

The walls built by Caesar two thousand years ago were built to walk on. As I went through one of the narrow archways, a fine young American asked to take my picture. It was my fortune that we met again, and he arranged to send me a copy. It was the wall he wanted; it was proof I had been there that I wanted.

The next day I had been up a long time before the boys came, so I was ready. Jerry and Tom were Christians, and I enjoyed their fellowship. We went through historic places and, circling Middlesbrough, we reached Durham Cathedral. It was a place the lieutenant had urged me to see; a fine example of Norman architecture.

Together we agreed to find Hadrian's Wall, built in A.D. 122, which crosses England from Newcastle to Carlyle. It was built to keep the warlike Picts of Caledonia, or Scotland, out of England. At Collerford we paid a fee and walked the wall for two hours. It was the highlight of my trip. I forgot my age as I accepted the challenge to keep up. The boys wore tennis shoes, and I had on Cuban heels, but my heels dug in and I went without mishap.

We drove on to Edinburgh, and I stayed at the Clifton Hotel. The boys found a place for themselves.

On the morning of Wednesday, May 27, 1964, I awoke to a foggy day in Edinburgh. I picked up a Gideon Bible and inscribed on the flyleaf was, "To the queen at her coronation . . . we present you with this book, the most valuable thing the world affords. Here is wisdom. This is the royal law. These are the oracles of God."

I studied a map over breakfast. When the boys came, we went to Edinburgh Castle where there were lifesize models of horses, each with its accouterments representing different eras of history. I was old enough to have lived when horses were the only means of land travel, and the statues thrilled me. Unfortunately, the castle gates were locked, and we were unable to go inside.

By now, for a reason I could not even surmise, the boys were in a tizzy to get going. I knew they were anxious about the ferry ride across the Firth of Forth, but there was something more important to them that I didn't know about.

The fog lifted as we ferried across the estuary of the North Sea. We were able to see for miles around. On the other side, we drove along the shore to St. Andrews. There I learned the reason for their anxiety.

St. Andrews was the location of the Royal and Ancient Golf Club, established in 1754. Tom and Jerry's greatest dream was to spend the day golfing on the course. They weren't sure I would be content to stay over a day while they had their fun, but I assured them that I would enjoy looking around without having to hurry. I would meet them at 7 p.m.

A Danish girl walked with me to St. Andrews University. There she showed me the famous Holm Oak, a great old tree, twisted and gnarled. There was also the ancient thorn tree said to have been planted by Mary Queen of Scots in the early 1400s. I managed to fill the day. A clock in the distance struck eight when the boys returned.

The next day they came for me at my hostel, and we went to St. John's Church in Perth. John Knox preached there during the Reformation.

For gifts to take home, the boys bought souvenir golf balls for their dads, and one bought a paperback version of the New Testament for his mother.

Traveling over the highlands, we looked for the monster at Loch Ness, and saw a sidewheel paddle steamer. We washed our hands in Loch Lomond. Scotland's beautiful rivers, lakes, rolling green hills, and grazing sheep reminded me of my beloved Oregon.

In Glasgow we found a room for me to settle in before my plane time. Jerry and Tom said good-bye, hoping we would meet again someday. My room was so cold that I paid to have the gas heater turned on and asked for a hot water bottle. I had to be warm or I would not sleep.

Friday, May 29, I woke up believing I would start home on this very day, even though my flight was scheduled for June 5. I packed my maps and brochures to mail home. I laid my Bible in my suitcase on top of my belongings and closed the lid. My money was almost gone and I needed to leave for home. I believed God was going to do something special to get me on a plane that day. I ate a good breakfast to be ready.

I went to More's Hotel, a block away, to get my ticket validated. I was told at the Icelandic desk that it was impossible to get a seat on the only flight that day. It was the Memorial weekend and they were booked solid.

I told the ticket agent I had to get on the plane. The reason was that I had run out of money. I was sure there would be a place for me. She sympathetically offered to give me some. I told her, "No, thank you, but I would like to have one of the 'large pennies' for use at the water closet." She laughed and gave me one.

She then encouraged me to go to the downtown desk and gave me a card with a map on it to help me find my way. When I arrived, I was told emphatically that there was no seat. I then took a bus to Renfro Airport. The plane was to leave at 9 p.m., and I was not about to give up.

When I asked about the flight, I found myself facing the same man I had talked to at the Icelandic office. He had driven to the airport to serve a shift at the desk there. Again he explained that my chances of getting a seat were hopeless.

In due time passengers began to file into their seats. Suddenly, the agent rushed over to me. "Lady, I don't know how you knew, but there is a 'no show.' Get through customs, you are on the flight."

With praise to the Lord, I followed the agent's orders. I never doubted that I was supposed to board that plane.

ENGLAND & SCOTLAND

Loch Ness

Perth
Dundee
St. Andrews
Firth of Forth

Loch Lomand

Glasgow
Edinburg

SCOTLAND

Newcastle

Carlisle

York

Nottingham

ENGLAND

Stratford
Upon Avon

Gloucester
London
Richmond
Bath
Dover
Southampton
Salisbury
Portsmouth

CHAPTER TEN

The Home Stretch

"Where no counsel is, the peope fall. . . ."
—Proverbs 11:14 (KJV)

At the international airport in New York City, the educated fingers of the inspector disdainfully identified the contents of my little suitcase. With contempt in his voice, he asked, "Didn't you bring back anything new with you?"

I answered meekly, "No, sir." Adroitly, he pushed the conveyer button and sent my suitcase into "outer darkness." On the other side of the checkpoint, I strapped it shut and tried to hurry. I was tired.

I took a limousine to the Greyhoud terminal, then a bus to a cloverleaf near the New Jersey Turnpike.

Because it was Memorial Day weekend, traffic was light. A young couple on their way to a Bible conference gave me a lift. When the man let me out, he palmed a five dollar bill into my hand and wished me Godspeed. I have an idea he had hitchhiked sometime himself. I accepted the money because I needed it.

My next ride was with a pleasant man in a very fine car. He let me out at the Bethlehem-Pennsylvania junction. Alone, I realized how exhausted I was. It was getting late, and I wondered where I would spend the night. Some time passed. Then, I noticed the man who had brought me to the junction walking toward me. His wife had sent him back to bring me home. They knew there would not be many rides because of the holiday weekend.

Mr. Martin (real names have not been used) was a corporate lawyer for a large company. They had a beautiful home, and as we arrived, the couple's son, a college student, also got home. After a brief introduction, he went upstairs to be alone. The man's wife was gracious. She knew how tired I was and insisted that I rest before we went to dinner.

She led me upstairs to a room with a canopied bed so high that it had steps to climb to get into it. She helped me out of my dress, removed my shoes and tucked me into bed. Kissing me on the forehead, she said, "You are out on your feet. Rest and I will come back for you." I slept for two hours.

We went to dinner, and a tour of the city followed. It was unbelievable the way they treated a stranger. That night I praised the Lord for the way He had met my needs.

The next day was Sunday. We all went to church, but we didn't go together. Gloria went to a small church she was in the habit of attending, and Mr. Martin took his son and me to a large church in town.

A young man who was a candidate for the position of youth pastor gave the message. The congregation was unaccustomed to his straightforward preaching and listened intently as he explained Acts 4:31. He said the apostles "spoke the Word with boldness" and that was what he would do.

"Being a church member is not enough to enter heaven. Works are not enough. . . . Do you have the Savior? Is He personal? . . . Are you put out on a limb?"

The lawyer's son's eyes were glued on the speaker as if he believed all that he heard. Mr. Martin never stirred. I was moved with a determination to be bold and do whatever God wanted me to do.

At the house again, two friends stopped by for brunch. By mid-afternoon, I realized that my hosts had been masking a problem of alcohol abuse and Gloria was drunk on beer. When the guests were gone, she asked Mr. Martin to help her to bed. "I don't want to be around when you quarrel," she said to him.

When he returned, he hardly knew what to say, but we did talk. I learned that his son had made himself obscure during the day before because he was afraid that, at some time, his mother's addiction would reveal itself. His son was ashamed.

The message at church that morning had channeled Mr. Martin's thoughts and he had concern for Gloria. By mid-afternoon, he had decided the time had come to help her.

I added that she was a wonderful, selfless woman. She had considered me out on the highway hoping for a ride that she knew might not come along and sent him back to get me. When Mr. Martin brought me home, she saw me looking my worst and put me to bed. I had lost a lot of weight, and I was exhausted. I cannot remember ever having been put to bed as tenderly as she put me. In all ways, she was a charming hostess. It hurt me to see her in her condition.

Mr. Martin offered that he had put his official position as a corporate lawyer ahead of his home and neglected to allow any time solely for his wife.

I doubt if a man in his position would have shared this with me, a perfect stranger, except that I had witnessed his wife's helplessness, heard the same sermon he did, and, perhaps, that I was older.

I left Monday morning and Mr. Martin wanted to pay my way home to Oregon. But I convinced him, beyond his understanding, that I wanted to hitchhike. He insisted that I could use the 20 dollars he gave me, and he was right about that. I had not expected that my money would not extend over the whole time of my trip. Lack of money was the reason I was home from Europe a week ahead of my schedule. I still believe, though, that "things don't just happen, they are planned."

I thanked Gloria for her gracious hospitality, and we said goodbye when she took me to the highway.

CHAPTER ELEVEN

Homeland

". . . My presence shall go with thee and
I will give thee rest."
                    —*Exodus 33:14 (KJV)*

I wanted to visit my offspring on the way home. It was June 1 when I arrived at my son Richard's in Detroit. When I left, he took me to the bus depot and gave me bus fare to go to Adrid's in Towanda, Illinois. As he kissed me goodbye, he said, "Mother, you can do anything you want, but I wish you would ride the bus."

I granted his wish and took the express bus going to Lincoln, Illinois. I knew it went through Towanda and stopped in Bloomington 20 miles beyond at a late hour. I didn't want to ask Adrid to get out of bed to come for me so I sat in the front seat and tried to persuade the driver to just slow down enough at Towanda for me to "jump out." He continually reminded me that he was instructed to let me off at Bloomington.

It began to rain, but the big windshield wipers allowed me to see where we were. It surprised me when the driver said in an aside, "Watch for the landmarks you know." When I named one, he slowed, stopped and opened the door. I descended near my daughter's house.

After a brief visit with Adrid and her family, I was back on the road. As I stood by a truckstop restaurant, a young black man inside recognized me and came out. He had grown up with my children. I was so glad to see him that I grabbed him by the shoulders and shook him. He grinned from ear to ear as he said, "One of the girls inside said there was an old woman out there hitchhiking, and I told them it could only be you."

My first ride was with a young Christian mother and her baby going to Lincoln. She said she had no opportunity for fellowship with other Christians, so we shared the things she wanted to talk about.

My next ride was one of the few times I have felt afraid. In a beautiful car, the driver drove through the city of Lincoln. He had another hitchhiker in the car, and when he let him out, he said we would stop at a motel. He was proud of himself and his lovely car. I guess he assumed I would be very impressed. Luke 10:19 came to my mind, ". . . *nothing shall by any means hurt you.*" The Lord filled my mouth with words to thwart the man's intentions which I promptly spoke. He stopped immediately and practically dumped me out on the highway.

Later, during the trip, I was trapped by a driver who took a side road, stopped, and made advances. I lifted one hand to the back of my hat and pulled out my long hatpin. I held it tightly, pointing it toward his face, telling him that if he didn't want some deep scars for the rest of his life, he had better let me go. When another car came into the side road and stopped, I was able to free myself. I rode in the second car to the main road, where I got another ride.

My next goal was Texas to see Eileen in Austin. A gentleman going to Dallas was glad for a passenger. We got a milkshake before we arrived in Joplin, Missouri. There, I stopped overnight at a hotel. The driver said he would come by the next morning if I wanted to ride on with him. When I woke in the morning and learned it was raining, I knew that the Lord had provided this ride for me. I would not get wet or be delayed.

At Dallas, the driver let me out at a bus stop so I could buy a ride to the edge of town. If the rides were right, I could make it to Eileen's that day.

Two young men stopped who were going to San Antonio. The passenger gave me his seat, moved to the back, and went to sleep.

The driver was interesting because he had traveled all over the world and by 9:30, he let me out at Eileen's house. I had come 600 miles and could give thanks.

Friday, June 5, was the day I was originally scheduled to leave

Glasgow, Scotland, and I was already in Texas. Eileen took me into custody. She took care of my clothes and took me to the hairdresser. We went shopping and finally to see my new great-granddaughter, who was born while I was overseas. Neighbors I had seen en route were glad to see me again. By the time the day ended, I was exhausted. Saturday and Sunday, I spent leisurely with family members as they came by.

I left Austin on Wednesday, making my way north with a variety of drivers to Mountain Home, Idaho, where Michal lived. She was the last grandchild to see on the trip. It was an early start from there on Friday as I headed toward Eugene, Oregon. When I got there I took a taxi on the last leg of the trip and by 3 a.m. I was settled in my little blue trailer.

Never to Europe? I had been to Europe!

CHAPTER TWELVE

Sandhill Cranes

"He that hath a bountiful eye shall be blessed. . . ."
—Proverbs 22:9 (KJV)

I got home on June 16. I had no job to return to, so I had time to rest and share my experiences. I had several small speaking engagements at women's organizations, and I dedicated a lot of time to typing the manuscripts of my trip. All of the postcards and pictures were placed into an album along with notes and captions. By the next spring I was ready for another excursion.

When I hiked the Alcan Highway in Alaska in 1954 and observed the breathtaking, migratory flight of the sandhill cranes, a desire was planted in me to know more about them. Eleven years had passed and it was April 1965. This was the year I had my 70th birthday.

I knew there was a bird refuge at Malheur Lake in Harney County in Eastern Oregon. I wrote to the Malheur National Wildlife Refuge at Burns and inquired about the cranes. The return letter pleased me. There were several hundred greater sandhill cranes at the refuge. There was a blind erected near the place preferred by the cranes, and I could observe them from there.

I was told to bring my sleeping bag, my food and cooking utensils. There was a building where I could camp. I was to go to Burns and from there telephone the refuge. They would work out my transportation.

To some folk, they would never have offered their rugged facilities, but I had sent a newspaper clipping about myself and told them of my modest mode of travel, so they did not hesitate to invite me. But my way of travel would be hampered. I had never carried a sleeping bag and I wondered whether anyone would pick me up, even though I was dressed like a lady.

Nevertheless, I loaded my barracks bag onto a city bus in Eugene and went to Thurston Road in Springfield, where I stood with the heap beside me. A logging truck came along and gave me a ride to Blue River. I told the driver about the Wyssen's Logging Company operation that had come over from Switzerland and their work in the Blue River area. He was so interested that he took me there to see some of the Swiss people I had met.

My rides came conveniently, and the last one was with a young man going beyond Burns. At 3 p.m., I made the phone call. Arrangements were made with Mrs. Jo White to meet me at a root beer stand. It was a scenic ride to Malheur.

It was dark and she showed me my shelter. When I was alone, I rolled out my sleeping bag on a table and put my groceries beside me. If there were mice, I didn't want to share with them.

"Whoo-oo, whoo-oo," demanded an owl on the roof at daybreak. I slid off the table and slipped outside to listen to the myriads of birds in their morning serenade. My heart echoed it.

I dressed and went to the office to introduce myself to Mr. Scharff, who had so kindly responded to my letter. I also met Mr. Harold Duebert. Then I went back and cooked breakfast on a round oak heater.

The headquarters was full of activity when I returned. Birds were being removed from a mist net for banding. There were birds, captive in a pond, where they could be easily observed. A raccoon, an animal destructive to nesting, was found in a trap. I took pictures and observed until lunchtime. Afterward, Mr. Duebert took me in a swamp buggy to Buena Vista Blind when he went on his route.

The size of the refuge and the many kinds of birds was more than I was prepared for. Pete French and other men of vision had claimed a lot of land for the birds. There were thousands of acres. Blitzen Valley was composed of small ponds, sloughs, and irrigated meadows. Sagebrush, juniper, and rock walls made borders. A metal watchtower built for the use of the refuge workers stood in full view. Buzzards used it for roosting.

The cranes flew away as we arrived, but I was thrilled at this first

Where I went to see the Sandhill Cranes. Malheur headquarters from "the pond."
The lookout tower I climbed is beyond. (April 28, 1965, Burns, Oregon)

glimpse of them. The blind was made of burlap fastened over a light wood frame. Mr. Duebert provided me with a fine pair of field glasses and left me there. It was two hours before the wary birds returned.

One crane evidently knew I was in the blind. He was the lookout. His eye was almost level with mine. The other birds fed in peace while he kept vigil.

I adjusted my camera to take a picture and waited to get the best shot. The lookout crane saw the half-inch movement of my finger and heard the tiny click. Just as fast, there was a wild lift and the cranes disappeared beyond the blue. It was another hour before they came back. I occupied myself watching Canada geese. When the cranes returned, I tried to get another picture. This time even the geese took off.

I had to be satisfied with observing. I was not ready to leave when the truck arrived for me.

The CCC mess hall was equipped with electricity. Two young reporters from the *Register-Guard* newspaper in Eugene were there, and they invited me to join them for supper. Mr. Scharff came to talk with them. That night the three of them slept on tables in the mess hall, and I learned the next morning that mice had been busy all around them.

This day, headquarters gave me a truck to go to Cole Island Dike for egret pictures. Back at night, I slept again on the uncomfortable table. My pleasure was immeasurable compared to the sleeping conditions.

Jo came early the next day to take me back to Burns. Harold Duebert took my picture and wished me happiness.

In Burns, I was interviewed by the editor of the *Times-Herald*, and my picture was taken again. It appeared in the paper May 13.

I ate breakfast and it was ten o'clock when I got out on the highway. A ride came an hour and 15 minutes later. It took me to Medford by way of one of the deepest precipices in the world, Albert Rim, in south central Oregon. I shall never forget it. My former boss at The Workman, Jim Petersen, lived in Medford. When I got there, I went to a pay phone at a gas station to call him. I reached his wife who sent him to get me. But, the gas station owner had already called the police to tell them that "an old hitchhiker is at my station." I was standing outside looking ladylike, except for my duffle bag, when the policemen came. Jim arrived at almost the same time and that helped settle any doubts about me. The Petersens served a very nice supper, and I had a good bed to sleep in again.

Jim set me out the next day on the ramp of Interstate 5. When I got to Sutherlin, it was starting to rain. A fine old Englishman in a California car, surprised to see a nicely-dressed lady standing by the road, stopped. "Darling, what are you doing standing in the rain?" He put my canvas bag and suitcase into the trunk and opened the door for me. We talked about England. He took me all the way to my trailer.

I kept in touch with John Scharff and his wife Florence at the refuge. In 1975, they wrote that reproduction of the cranes had not been good. In 1985, a note stated, "The flooding in the valley has ruined the refuge beyond . . . the road into headquarters is under three feet of water."

[Author's note: Currently, 1989, much has been restored. Flood waters have receded due to less snow pack in the mountains and recent dry seasons. The old road is open again to the game refuge and reproduction of the sandhill cranes is on the increase.]

CHAPTER THIRTEEN

Unshackled

"According to Thy name, O God, so is Thy praise
unto the ends of the earth. . . ."
—Psalm 48:10 (KJV)

Whenever I hiked, something always happened to remind me of God's faithfulness. I had been visiting in Sacramento and was ready to go home. I felt I should start early, so before daybreak a friend took me to the junction of Highways 40 and 99.

Under the dim vapor light, my grey coat was hard to see, and I was concerned about getting a ride very soon. I also had an uneasiness as if some evil was forthcoming. I strengthened myself by thinking on my morning verse from Psalm 131, *". . . hope in the Lord from henceforth and forever."*

Several cars passed me by and then I noticed that one from Sacramento went as far as the curve and the lights shut off. The driver turned slowly and pulled off the road into the weeds. He drove back off of the highway and stopped just beyond where I stood. It would be untruthful to say I was not frightened.

"Hope in the Lord" came as real as if someone had spoken it. At the same time, a car came along and stopped for me.

"Get in," the driver said reluctantly. As I shut the door he continued, "I sure don't know why I stopped for you. I just don't pick up hitchhikers any more."

There was a brief pause before he explained. "The last time I picked up a hitchhiker, it cost me over $100. I paid a $25 fine, a $25 tow bill, and lost over $50 in wages. . . . I just don't stop anymore," he emphasized. "I don't know why I stopped for you."

I didn't tell him. He explained it was for his own sake he was letting me out at Woodland.

There, I walked to the north end of town because I knew the walk would do me good. I stood by a gas station where I had stood so many times before and that amused me.

Traffic was slow, so I took a ride I would not ordinarily have taken, but it was alright. The man was out of work and had been hunting for a job in the oil fields. I paid him $2 to ride as far as Redding where he hoped to make some contacts. He was not able to reach anyone there, so he chose to keep on going.

I wondered why I was still with this man; he had nothing positive to say and that irritated me. He was uptight; I could not figure him out. One good thing, he treated me with respect like the grandmother I was.

By the time we got to Cottage Grove, his troubles just poured out. The years totaled many that he had not talked about his unhappy childhood. Now, he trusted an old woman when he would not have trusted a "holier than thou" preacher, let alone a "formally trained social worker." It really surprised me.

I was able to share my childhood with him and how I grew up like a boy in Cooksville. That helped me to communicate. I told him about my faith in God, too.

Finally, he seemed to have hope and began to talk positively. I knew then why I had started hitchhiking before daybreak. "Things don't just happen; they are planned."

He took me to my trailer home in Eugene.

CHAPTER FOURTEEN

My Thumb

". . . for I shall yet praise Him who is the health of my countenance, and my God."

—Psalm 43:5 (KJV)

I have often looked at my right thumb and laughed at its sharp outward curve. It was made for hitchhiking. In my only baby picture, my thumb appears ready to hitch as my right arm is outstretched on my lap. Though my hiking at first was an escape, and later my purposes were for family, historical places and sightseeing, my greatest joy was when I had opportunities to speak for the Lord.

I could fill another book with stories about traveling in the States after I was 70 and into my 80s. This excerpt took place near Cambria, California, while I was on my way to see Hearst's Castle.

I was standing beside the road and had not yet put up my thumb when a state patrol car pulled over in front of me. Inside were two stalwart officers. Next, a county sheriff's car pulled up behind me. There were two officers inside.

These two cars, with four large men, had stopped for a 5' 5½," 135-pound, properly dressed old woman standing on a ramp who had not indicated she was hitchhiking. I felt like a David with four Goliaths.

An officer from the front car went to confer with the officers in the car behind me. I quit standing and walked to the officer left alone. I thought I could handle "one on one." I showed him a clipping of a recent story about me in the Lompoc newspaper of January 18, 1966, along with my picture.

At Griffith Observatory overlooking Los Angeles, California, January 24, 1965. (Courtesy of Jack Allen)

He looked at it and laughed because it referred to areas that "take a dim view of hitchhikers."

By this time the conference behind me was over and the verdict was what I hoped for.

One car took me out of the county's jurisdiction to a 35-mile-per-hour zone where it was safe. "Stand here. You will soon get a ride."

Another time, after I was 70, I took an extensive trip job hunting. I wanted to supplement my $70 Social Security check. Visiting relatives along the way, I went as far as San Diego without success.

The first day I was encouraged by words from Deuteronomy 10:12: *"Fear the Lord . . . walk, love, serve, keep they heart."*

I set out to take Highway 58. There a man passed me in a pick-up, turned around and came back. He told me the highway was closed and offered to take me to Goshen Junction so I could go south on Highway 99. That day my trusty thumb stopped ten people. They each had a story that prompted me to tell of God's goodness to me.

Job hunting took me further to the home of my cousins, Gwen Mills Van Zant and her husband Lonnie, in Maxwell, New Mexico. From there, I decided to extend my trip as far as Eileen's in Austin, Texas.

When I arrived, I had a cold and my eyes burned miserably. I rested several days, praying and asking the Lord what He wanted me to do next.

On February 25, I set out for Illinois. It was a day I called a "skate day," because everything was frozen.

It took nine rides to get to Durant, Oklahoma. Every conversation was eternally valuable to at least one of us.

When I arrived in Bloomington, Illinois, Adrid came and took me to her home in Towanda. She wanted me to stay and buy a little house that was for sale nearby. I went to see it, but decided against buying. I could not settle down.

By this time, my arrival as the "Hitchhiking Grandmother" was newsworthy, and neighbors, Ken and Jan Trotter, phoned the *Bloomington Pantagraph*. I was interviewed and my picture was taken. The story appeared March 11.

I left for the West again and took a bus part of the way, but I hitched numerous rides through Iowa, Colorado, Utah, Nevada, and Oregon. I was back home in Eugene by March 16.

I do not believe I was supposed to get a job; I believe I was supposed to encourage people and tell of God's faithfulness. And one thing I know for certain: I could not have done it if my mind had not been renewed daily by reading the Bible and having time in prayer at the beginning of each day.

I will never know the results of my witnessing, speaking for the Lord, but I know that: "Nothing just happens. It is planned." Even when I put up my thumb.

My travel albums, manuscripts and family history stacked in one place (1986).

CHAPTER FIFTEEN

My Last Trip

"Return unto thy rest, O my soul, for the Lord hath dealt bountifully with thee."

—Psalm 116:7 (KJV)

I was at my daughter Hazel's home in Washington when I was in my 80s and had a serious fall. I spent some time in a nursing home before I went back to my home in Oregon. Though it would have made my children happy if I had given up living alone at this time, I chose to go home to be near my telephone where I could visit with my friends. I also wanted to have ready access to my 83 travel albums. I was used to looking at some of them every day. I was an avid reader, and when I couldn't go to the library to get books, the Eugene Public Library book-mobile brought books to my home. My neighbors came by and took me to church. My friend, Thelma Peck, faithfully sent out my Christmas letters for me each year. I started them in 1964 and she sent the last one in 1985. I was not ready to give up.

At the age of 91, I had a minor fall in my trailer home. A trip to the hospital and a stay at a nursing home until I was able to travel, preceded my going to live with my daughter Eileen in Austin, Texas. Hazel accompanied me by plane. My manuscripts and albums were stored in Washington. It had to come to this sometime.

Thoughts of my life from the time I was a child in Cooksville, through all of the years since then, pass through my mind. I have so much to be thankful for. I had good health. There were people who came into my life to enrich it and without them my life would have had little meaning. I learned to have faith, ambition and determination.

196

My 93rd birthday. Eileen's daughter, Leslie, stands by. Austin, Texas, September 21, 1988. (Courtesy of Eileen Baker)

I could call this period now a fourth life, because the other three phases are past, but time is too short for that. Old age is like babyhood; it doesn't last long.

However, this trip to Austin is not my last trip. I have one more trip to take, and it won't be by plane, and I won't have to indicate that I need a ride by using this old curved thumb.

"That" Grace

About The Author

Writer Ruth Barton Davis met Grace Small, the "hitchhiking grandmother," in 1985 when a mutual friend introduced them in Eugene, Oregon, with the prospect that they might collaborate in writing Grace's autobiography. Because the writer and the adventurer shared common perspectives about life and spiritual values, they made a match and agreed to produce the book together. Over a period of four years, they met together, corresponded and talked by phone as the manuscript was drafted and finally prepared for publication.

Ruth Davis was born in Grants Pass, Oregon, in 1920, one of 11 children. She began writing in high school and published her first poetry in Eugene High School's literary publication *Eidolon*. In the 1970s, she wrote travel stories about her trips to Maine and Baja, Mexico. After joining The Writers Support Group at the Eugene Public Library in 1984, she wrote a number of poems and short stories and published several articles including: "A Beautiful Cup of Soup" for *MaineSay,* a statewide Gannett publication for mature living in Maine; and "Prepare Harvest Bounty for Winter Meal Rewards" for *Senior*

News, an Oregon monthly published by Phoenix Senior World, Inc. In addition, she has illustrated one of her poems—"Mars Hill Mountain" with a painting that is being prepared for commercial sales in Maine coast gift shops.

She taught high school in Maine and Oregon before she married Harold J. Davis in 1948. Together they reared five children at their country home near Junction City in the heart of Oregon's fertile Willamette Valley. The Davises ran a television and appliance business for 17 years.

The author has traveled in the United States and Canada extensively and also spent time in Baja, Mexico. She is an artist and published poet and sings with a group in the First Baptist Church in Junction City.

Most of her friends and readers characterize Ruth Davis's personality and work as being most influenced by her positive attitude toward life and a spontaneous sense of humor.